BREAKING
YOUR
ADDICTION
HABIT

BREAKING
YOUR
ADDICTION
HABIT

With Amino Acids and Nutrient Therapy

by

Billie Jay Sahley, Ph.D., and

Katherine M. Birkner, C.R.N.A., Ph.D.

Pain & Stress Therapy Center Publication
San Antonio, Texas
1990

Note to Readers

This material is not intended to replace services of a physician, nor is it meant to encourage diagnosis and treatment of illness, disease, or other medical problems by the layman. This book should not be regarded as a substitute for professional medical treatment and while every care is taken to ensure the accuracy of the content, the authors and the publisher cannot accept legal responsibility for any problem arising out of experimentation with the methods described. Any application of the recommendations set forth in the following pages is at the reader's discretion and sole risk. If you are under a physician's care for any condition, he or she can advise you as to whether the programs described in this book are suitable for you.

This publication has been compiled through research resources at **The Pain & Stress Therapy Center**, San Antonio, Texas 78229.

First Edition
Printed in the U.S.A.

A Pain & Stress Therapy Center Publication
Edited by Evett & Associates, San Antonio, Texas
Cover Design by Accutype of San Antonio
Typesetting & Printing by First Impressions of San Antonio

Additional copies may be ordered from:
The Pain & Stress Therapy Center
5282 Medical Drive, Suite 160, San Antonio, Texas 78229-6043

Library of Congress Catalog Card Number 90-60548

ISBN

There is no such thing as an impossible dream.
If you believe it, you can make it happen.

Acknowledgements

Our sincere appreciation and thanks to:

The staff of The Pain & Stress Therapy Center of San Antonio, Texas (past and present) for their support and dedication to helping people with addiction problems.

Antonio L. Ruiz, M.D., Medical Director of The Pain & Stress Therapy Center for his support, encouragement, and guidance.

Doris Rapp, M.D., Buffalo, New York, one of God's gifted healers, and an inspiration and a leader to physicians, therapists, and educators.

Max V. Ricketts, Jr., for all of his help, wealth of information and research, and friendship.

The many physicians across the country using orthomolecular medicine who share their research and give us constant encouragement.

Our patients, who teach us something everyday.

Contents

Introduction 1
I What Is Drug Addiction? 4
   Trends in Substance Abuse
     Alcohol—Tobacco—Marijuana—Heroin—
     Methadone—Barbiturates—Minor
     Tranquilizers—Amphetamines—Cocaine—
     LSD and Other Hallucinogens—Inhalants
II Withdrawal and Recovery 18
    Recovery Time—The Need for Detoxification—
    Reduction Procedures—Anxiety—Medication—
    Withdrawal Procedure—Esterified C—
    Allergic Reactions
III Alcoholism and Its Treatment 34
     Progression of Drinking Symptoms—Symptoms
     of Alcohol Withdrawal (Mild)—Symptoms of
     Alcohol Withdrawal (Late)—Metabolism of
     Alcohol—Factors Leading to Malnutrition in
     Alcoholism—Alcohol/Drug-Induced
     Nutritional Deficiencies—Treatment
IV Nicotine and Caffeine Addiction and Treatment . . . 46
    Nicotine—Caffeine
V Amino Acids for Therapy 53
   Branch Chain Amino Acids—GABA—
   L-Glutamine, The Surprising Brain Fuel—
   Phenylalanine—Neuropharmacology of
   Synapses of Pain—Inhibitory Pathway—
   DLPA and Depression—L-Tyrosine—
   L-Tryptophan—L-Cystine—L-Carnitine—
   Taurine
Footnotes 101
Bibliography 110
Index 117

Tables

Amino Acids and Nutrients Used for Recovery   17
   from Substance Abuse Dependency on a Daily Basis
Amino Acids and Their Effect on The Body   85
Drug-Nutrient Interactions   87
Amino Acids and Clinical Conditions   88
   and Diseases
Symptoms of Vitamin Deficiencies   90
Dietary Precursors and Effects   100

Introduction

O**rthomolecular Therapy** means supplying the cells with the right mixture of nutrients. Many diseases are known to be the result of the wrong balance of essential nutrients in the body. Adjusting the diet, eliminating junk foods, and ingesting the proper doses of essential vitamins, minerals, and amino acids can correct the chemical imbalance of disease.

The orthomolecular approach helps patients become more aware of our dangerously polluted environment and nutrient-stripped refined foods. This approach is both corrective and preventive. Meganutrient therapy has become a part of orthomolecular medicine. While it is becoming widely recognized that orthomolecular therapy cures patients by correcting body chemistry imbalances, it is not widely known that in certain combinations, meganutrients can be as immediately effective as potent painkillers or tranquilizers.

Meganutrients treat the whole person's biochemical imbalances; they can be of immediate and long-term benefit. The type of treatment offered by ortho-molecular doctors and therapists varies, but the mainstream of work focuses upon meganutrient therapy and diagnostic tests, and treatment with adequate

nutrients is a distinguishing characteristic of orthomolecular medicine.

Orthomolecular therapy takes into consideration
that every individual is biochemically unique. Every
patient has a different nutrient and amino acid requirement, and with application of this therapy each individual's need is met and the mind and body achieve a
state of homeostasis—a condition where everything in
the body is in balance and capable of resisting
environmental changes, while regulating internal
metabolic function.

Every tissue of the body is affected by nutrition.
Under conditions of poor nutrition the kidneys stop
filtering, the stomach stops digesting, the adrenals stop
secreting, and other organs follow suit.

Good nutrition is essential to the preservation of
health and prevention of disease—especially with
respect to the question of optimum intake of essential
vitamins, minerals, and amino acids.

Orthomolecular therapy is both corrective and
preventive. Meganutrient therapy has become a part of
orthomolecular medicine, which has continually
expanded and now recognizes that all of our biological
interactions with food, water, air, and light are an important part of good health and the prevention of illness
if they are taken in the proper amounts.

IMPORTANT WARNING:

RX DRUGS ARE **DRUGS**

There are no drugs in pharmacology which cure anxiety, panic, phobias, insomnia, depression, allergies, arthritis, asthma, cardiac, diabetes, hypertension, hyperactivity, or inflammatory conditions, pain, or disease.

There are many drugs which treat the <u>symptoms</u> of these disorders. However, many prescription drugs have a significant potential for long-term adverse or permanent drug side-effects.

When the word "addict" is used, it does not mean just the addict on street drugs. What it does mean is people from all walks of life, all ages, whole families. Even children are not immune if their parents allow them to take prescribed drugs such as antidepressants, tranquilizers, or stimulants; this, in fact, sets up a pattern for a lifetime with a chemical straight-jacket.

I
What is
Drug Addiction?

Addictions affect one out of three people. In the United States alone, more than ten million people are affected by the use of some type of toxic substance. It is well established that tranquilizers, antidepressants, pain medication, substance abuse, and alcohol constitute a major health problem in the U.S. Approximately 200,000 men, women, and children will die prematurely every year from a wide range of prescription drugs, alcohol, and substance related problems and illnesses including cancer, heart disease, suicide, and homicide, as well as highway fatalities and other other accidents. Addictions can and do affect people from all social classes, of all degrees of intelligence, and all professional levels.

According to the President's Commission on Mental Health, a fourth of the citizens in the U.S. suffer from some type of severe emotional stress. Another study shows that 80 percent of all Americans feel the need to reduce stress in their daily lives. All the available information points to the fact that people want to understand the forces of stress and the effect it has on their mind and body, and explore the use of amino acids for pain, stress, and anxiety.

A cry for help from the American public has gone out: how can they reduce the harmful impact of stress on their physical and mental well-being? Many have come to expect instant relief from emotions and negative feelings, and find it necessary to look for instant pleasure that is chemically induced. Given this information, records show that drugs—and a greater inclination to try them, once or twice or perhaps sporadically—fit conveniently into our stress-filled society. These substances allow the manipulation of moods by simply providing an escape for the user.

All substances of abuse either elevate or decrease consciousness and intensifies depressed moods. Escape is the primary factor, and the drug of choice will be the one the user feels will give him instant relief. A person who is addicted will always have to satisfy his addiction before he can move on to do anything else.[1] Everyone has problems and the anti-depressants, tranquilizers, pain pills, drugs, and alcohol make one feel these problems are not pressing...that you can put your worries and your life on hold. But prescription drugs and alcohol make problems unmanageable, unresolvable, and unbearable. Prescription drug and street drug users are thirty times more likely to commit suicide than the norm.

What predisposes a person to choose a particular substance? It is their availability through prescriptions or contacts, and finding the funds to pay for it. This is especially evident among teens and those even younger.[2] We live in an addictive society, a society that has all the characteristics and exhibits all the effects of the alcoholic or prescription addict.

As healthcare professionals who work with addiction know, the most caring thing we can do is not to embrace the denial, but confront the disease. The primary cause of the addict's problem is not psychological illness, but physical addiction. An addiction is any process over which we are powerless. Prescription drugs, street drugs, and alcohol take control of a person, causing him to do and think things that are inconsistent with his personal values. It leads him to become more compulsive and obsessive.[3]

A particular symptom of an addiction is the sudden need for the addict to destroy himself and others. He often lies, denies, and covers-up. The addictive personality feels compelled to lie and is unwilling to give anything. He is unaware of what is going on inside of him. He does not have to deal with his anger, pain, depression, confusion, or even joy and love; he does not have these feelings, or feels them only vaguely. The addicted person stops relying on his knowledge and sense and relies on confused perceptions. During this time there is a lack of internal awareness that deadens his internal processes, which in turn allows him to remain addicted. The addicted person loses contact with himself and with other people around him.

An addictive substance dulls and distorts sensory input and output. The user does not receive information clearly nor does he process it correctly. He is unable to assimilate feedback information or respond to it accurately. Since addicts are not in touch with themselves, they present a distorted self to the world. Addicts con people and eventually lose the ability to become intimate with others, even those they are closest to and love most—their family and their friends.

Addicts are aware that something is very wrong, but the addictive thinking tells them that it could not possibly be their fault. This kind of thinking also tells them that they cannot make things right—that someone else will have to do it for them. An addiction absolves the users from having to take responsibility for their lives, and permits the assumption that someone or something outside themselves will swoop down to make things better or help them deal with what they are going through. Since addicts tend to be dependent and feel increasingly powerless and bad about themselves, the notion that they can take responsibility for their lives is inconceivable to them.

The longer the addict waits to be rescued, the worse the addiction becomes. Regardless of what they are addicted to, it takes more and more to create the desired effect, and no amount is ever enough! Before being ready for recovery, the individual alcohol/addict must hit bottom. At this time a new sense of reality surfaces: they no longer want to hide their addiction, they want help.

Addictions can be divided into two major categories:

1) addiction to substances such as alcohol, prescription and street drugs, nicotine, caffeine, and food, and

2) addictions to processes such as gambling and shopping.

For the addict to come to terms with the possibility that he could be addicted to both, and therefore must recover from both, is staggering. According to Alcoholics Anonymous, the addicted person cannot remain static; he must either get better or worse. Both addiction and recovery are processes.

The addicted personality is one that has been enslaved—a prisoner of his own mind, condemned by his own guilt, fear, and fear of failure. This is one of the reasons he must hit bottom before he admits he is out of control and needs help with his fears—fear of living, fear of loss of control. The addict must not concern himself with how he got there, only with recovery, living one day at a time. He cannot allow fear of the future to set in, as this leads to almost certain failure. An addict grieves for the past and all of the time he wasted, the people he hurt, the lives he destroyed. But his fear of the future brings forth a new set of problems, anxieties, fears, and phobias. Now he must become responsible and face the realities he has avoided, denied, and pushed aside.

The most important and enduring part of the global response to the addiction problem has been intellectual. Substance abuse therapists and researchers around the world have sought to understand why people try to escape through the use of drugs and alcohol, as well as the long-term negative effects on the brain.

Researchers have found that there is a specific

receptor in the brain for morphine. Shortly thereafter, it was discovered that there were natural brain chemicals that fit these receptors. This finding opened the door to a new understanding of the psychiatric profile of substance abusers and their brain function.

Researchers have determined there is a neuro-chemical imbalance that makes the alcoholic incapable of drinking normally. His body simply does not process alcohol correctly. And unlike other psychoactive drugs, alcohol does not target specific parts of nerve cells or neurons but seems to enter cell membranes and sabotage the nervous system indiscriminately.

The National Institute of Mental Health is studying how alcohol affects certain cells in the brain to induce a sedative effect. The complex workings of the brain provide a map with unique pathways for the addicted. Although some become sedated, others become agitated, angry, depressed and melancholy, anxious, excited, and fearful. The brain chemistry holds the key. Deficiencies or imbalances are thought to be the result of genetic anomalies, metabolic disturbances due to stress, or the destructive effects of prescription drugs, alcohol, or drug abuse.

One theory on addiction, according to Janice Phelps, M.D., is that it is due to a biochemical defect with which certain individuals are born. The physiologic flaw begins at least in part in the adrenal glands. This defect consists of a sugar imbalance or dysmetabolism and a chronic biochemical depression or genetic depression. Genetic depression is a chronic physiological and biochemical depression that is passed from generation to generation in some families, though not necessarily affecting all family members. Genetic depression is very closely related to addictiveness, conceivably arising from the same physiological defect in the brain.

Genetic depression may arise in infancy or child-hood, or it may not appear until the teen years or even adulthood. It may go unrecognized if it has been present so long that for that person it seems normal; the person living with it has become an expert at concealing it.

The signs of genetic depression are many and varied. Signs of this imbalance in infants are indigestion or stomachaches. In older children, it might be manifested as anxiety, learning disabilities, attention problems, or hyperactivity. In the adult, headaches, backaches, and stomachaches are common, as are anxiety and worry. Sleep disorders, appetite changes, lack of energy, and constant fatigue may also be present. Even changes in sexual response may be related to depression. A defect in the chemical communication from the brain to the adrenals seems to provide the single key.

The signs and symptoms of depression must be recognized,[4] but anxiety and depression are so similar at times that even physicians cannot tell the difference.[5] The relationship between the pituitary-adrenal axis and depression must be understood. Some of the major symptoms include physical pain and symptoms, perhaps even mental illness in the genetically depressed person. With the underlying addictiveness or family history of addiction, many symptoms may be attributed to depression. Many addicted people do not realize they are depressed and have been depressed all of their lives.

According to Dr. Phelps, a good working definition of addiction is as follows: "An addiction is the compulsive and out-of-control use of any chemical substance that can produce recognizable and identifiable unpleasant withdrawal symptoms when use of the substance is stopped. Such addiction is driven by an inborn physiological hunger in the addictive person, and is frequently intimately related to depression."

All addicting substances, from sugar to nicotine to narcotics, seem to give short-term relief from depression in the beginning. Later, the same substance aggravates it. The authors believe the degree of "normalcy," "relaxation," or feeling of well-being a person experiences from an addicting substance probably is related to the subject's degree of depression. There is no doubt that a link exists between depression and addiction. It plays an important role in the overall pattern of addiction and addictive behavior.[6]

No one ever fully recovers from anxiety, insomnia, or depression while on drugs, whether the drugs are in the form of alcohol, street dope, or pharmaceutical-grade drugs.

Millions of dollars are spent publicizing and promoting pharmaceuticals rather than researching them. The promotions are to convince all of us that the prescription products are useful and beneficial so that physicians will prescribe them and the public will request them. The pharmaceutical industry thrives on illness, not on wellness; it has no significant financial motivation to strive for wellness in society. Sick days pay, not well days.

Most physicians are unappreciative of the extent nutrition plays in wellness. Many psychiatrists live under the illusion that anything below the brain cannot contribute to an emotionally healthy person—and amino acids and nutrients do not count. Most doctors' education regarding nutrition is only superficial and generally is limited to one semester in medical school. The greatest part of their nutrition education deals with caloric requirements and the recommended daily allowances. The recommended daily allowances are simply the bare minimum nutritional requirements to prevent the onset of states of deficiency. Yet a whole new world of healing awaits them with nutritional medicine.

The late Carl C. Pfeiffer, M.D., Ph.D., renowned for his work in the field of orthomolecular medicine, summed up the challenge in what he calls "Pfeiffer's Law," which states, "We have found that if a drug can be found to do the job of medical healing, a nutrient can be found to do the same job. When we understand how a drug works, we can imitate its action with one of the nutrients."

The pharmaceutical giants in the early sixties began marketing a new class of drugs called the benzodiazepines or "minor" tranquilizers/sedatives. This was done to meet the commercial demands for anxiety relief. The most popular trade names of this class are Xanax, Valium, Tranxene, Halcion, Librium, Ativan, Dalmane,

Loxitane, and Librax.

Benzodiazepines are available as commercial products, but they do not cure anxiety, depression, stress, or insomnia. These drugs exist because of the tremendous profits they generate for the pharmaceutical companies that manufacture and promote them.[7] These companies spend millions entertaining physicians to convince them to prescribe these products. The resulting profits are made possible by the inherent addictive potential of these drugs and the patent protection of the drug manufacturers who hold exclusive rights for seventeen years. Thus, when users become dependent on particular drugs, the pharmaceutical companies stand to make huge profits.

A condition which baffles many drug victims is characterized by free-floating anxiety and panic attacks. These attacks, can come without warning and seemingly without reason.[8] This sends the poor, anxiety-ridden and confused person to the nearest emergency room. After admission, every conceivable test is administered; the physicians determine the cause is actually a panic and/or an anxiety attack which can take on the symptoms of a heart attack.[9] Thirty percent of admissions in the emergency rooms in the United States are actually panic/anxiety attacks disguised as heart attacks.[10]

Prescription drug dependents become addicts in large measure because they are unaware of natural alternatives and orthomolecular therapy. They make choices based on the convention that has taught them to trust their doctor and his medicines. These victims go through a long period of addiction denial. But denial is self-defeating. Addicts, and often their families as well, deny the addiction. Many never do admit it and never look at the situation honestly; it is too frightening for them to do so. Honest, open communication or feelings in a non-judgemental way is vital to breaking an addiction.[11]

There appears to be agreement about the presence of the three major elements in the drug abuse problem: the drugs, the people who use them, and the social forces shaping, and in turn being influenced by, both of these. A recently coined term that fits the study of all three of these elements is "social pharmacology"; it now awaits new definitions and delineations of its role in the psychotropic (i.e., acting on the mind) drug abuse field. From the enormous number of studies that provide some answers to the question of how widespread is drug and alcohol use, several tentative conclusions may be drawn. Marijuana appears to attract the greatest experimentation and narcotics the least, with other drugs falling in between. Males tend to experiment more than females; persons who are better educated and with higher incomes tend to "try out" drugs more frequently than persons who are less educated and have lower incomes. Dr. Kenneth Blum, a pharmacologist, has shown the comparison of drug abuse with recreational drugs; he reveals that lack of consistency in society's approach to both. A person may be a confirmed alcoholic and be regarded as "sick" in our society. But one who habitually uses marijuana and is dependent on it psychologically will be viewed as a criminal, not a sick person, even if the social liability of both individuals is much the same. The attitude of many people is that society does not need either one: we already have ten million alcoholics, so why create a comparable class of addicts?

This attitude characterizes the thinking of the American public. Even drugs prescribed by a physician may not be good for you, and serious side effects as well as long-term addiction can occur. Those with emotional problems and chronic pain are potential victims of this, "it's okay to take" attitude. The Council on Patient Information and Education states, "Up to half of all prescription drugs are taken incorrectly."

Trends in Substance Abuse

Alcohol
More than nine million people are believed to have a

definite problem with alcohol. The past fifteen years have shown a 30 percent increase in alcohol consumption.

Tobacco

Tobacco is second to alcohol in its widespread use. Fifty-five million Americans smoke cigarettes daily. It is estimated that more than 300,000 people die prematurely each year from illnesses related to smoking. Currently, about 22 percent of youths and 40 percent of adults are regular smokers.

Marijuana

Cannabis is the most commonly used illegal drug. The rates are highest among the 18 to 25 year olds, but its use is spreading to those younger and older. Ten percent of high school seniors are daily users. The most common adverse reaction to marijuana is a state of acute anxiety, sometimes accompanied by paranoid thoughts.

Heroin

The number of those addicted to heroin has stabilized during the past few years at about a half million people. Heroin potency in street material is down to 5 percent, and the cost per pure milligram of heroin has risen to about two dollars. The increased price and decreased potency are believed to reflect a diminished availability.

Methadone

Methadone has become a drug of abuse through its use as a maintenance treatment for about 80,000 users. Since it is effective for about 24 to 36 hours during maintenance therapy, take-home supplies are given to those patients who are allowed to visit a clinic only two or three times a week.

Barbiturates

The source of black market barbiturates and other

hypnotics is usually from prescription drugs but they are supplemented with illegitimately manufactured products.

Minor Tranquilizers
In 1987, ninety million prescriptions for minor tranquilizers were filled; there was a slight decrease from the previous year. One fourth of all drug-related emergency room visits are connected with tranquilizer usage.

Amphetamines
Amphetamines and other appetite-suppressant prescription drugs account for almost seventeen million prescriptions in 1987. Reports available show they were used for narcolepsy, minimal brain dysfunction, and (in short courses) weight control. The level of abuse is holding steady. Amphetamines remain a potential item of increased abuse.

Cocaine
Cocaine use continues to increase, with most of those who indulge doing so sporadically. This pattern may be due to its high cost and relative availability. The abuse of this drug is expected to increase during the next few years.

LSD and Other Hallucinogens
LSD. DMT, and other hallucinogenic drugs have declined in use since the mid 1960's, but they have by no means disappeared from the drug scene. Use of PCP or "angel-dust" is on the increase; the results of its ingestion concern healthcare professionals and law enforcement officials. The person under the influence of PCP is more apt to engage in unpredictable, violent behavior than has been encountered with other hallucinogens. The individual may present a variety of neurologic and psychiatric toxic reactions that are not easily diagnosed or treated.

Inhalants

The sniffing of commercial products containing solvents or the contents of aerosol sprays is a juvenile practice that does not always terminate when one becomes an adult. The practice is on the increase. Sudden sniffing death and chronic organ damage have been documented with the use of aerosol sprays.[12]

Drug dependence should be viewed as a persistence beginning from a low degree of dependence seen in social or experimental usage, and ranging to physical dependency or addiction. Drug dependence or addiction can be considered from two aspects: one relates to the interaction between the drug and the individual; the other to the interaction between the drug abuse and society—environmental, sociological, and economic. Investigation of drug abuse is currently proceeding along these two areas as well as the interaction of the two dimensions.

In conclusion, two questions must be answered:
1. What brain chemicals are possibly in excess or deficit in the potential addict?
2. What biological markers exist that can help in predicting high-risk groups or individuals?

Consensus in research matters reveals that certain mental states such as depression and schizophrenia are caused in part by a deficit of norepinephrine and an excess of dopamine, respectively. Additionally, there are theories describing deficits of brain internal opiates called endorphins occurring in compulsive diseases such as alcohol and drug-seeking behavior.

AMINO ACIDS AND NUTRIENTS THAT CAN BE USED FOR RECOVERY FROM SUBSTANCE ABUSE DEPENDENCY ON A DAILY BASIS

Nutrient	Amount	Therapeutic Action	Behavior Change
L-Tyrosine	2,000-3,000 mg spread throughout day	Increases norepine-phrine, dopamine	Anti-anxiety, Anti-stress, Antidepressant
Tryptophan (When available)	2,000 mg AM & PM	Precursor loading Decreases pain and depression	Anti-craving Reduces Insomnia
Glutamine	3,000 mg (1,000 mg 3 times per day)	Precursor loading	Anti-craving Anti-stress
Niacinamide	1,000 mg AM & PM	Enzyme co-factor	Decreases pain and depression Speeds up neurotransmitters
P 5 P or Pyridoxal-5-Phosphate	10-20 mg	Promotes absorption of amino acids	Facilitates neurotransmitters
B Complex	100 mg	Assists action of amino acids	
GABA	3,000 mg/ daily spread throughout day. Use as free-form.	Fills GABA receptors	Anti-anxiety
Esterified C	3-5,000 mg spread throughout day	Facilitates action of nutrients and amino acids	Anti-oxidant Anti-toxin
Multi-Vitamin (Good)	1 daily	Provides minimum daily requirement.	

Nutrient	Amount	Therapeutic Action	Behavior Change
DLPA 750	2 daily	Helps keep endorphin level and mood up. Helpful with chronic pain.	Mood elevation Pain relief
Ginkgo Biloba	120 mg daily	Enhances memory after drug use	
Gymnema Sylvestre	1-2 caps 15 minutes prior to meals	Helps to decrease sugar craving	
Siberian Ginseng	1-2 caps daily	Adaptogenic herb that is used in conjunction with amino acids	Anti-stress
BCAA (Branch Chain Amino Acids)	2 daily	Provides necessary amino acids for recovery	
B A M	2 daily	Provides essential amino acids in balanced formula	

II
Withdrawal and
Recovery

Many of the symptoms experienced by those who want to withdraw from an addiction are anxiety related simply because of increasing uncertainty about whether they will succeed. Withdrawal reactions will vary a great deal from person to person. Some people can reduce the quantity and even drop tranquilizers without any problems, others have minor problems, and some have major withdrawal problems. **Caution must be taken by those who want to withdraw. You should not begin withdrawal unless you follow a program that advises you on how and what to do and what to expect.**

Withdrawal and recovery take time. Addiction does not happen overnight and your system cannot release all the accumulated toxins at once. There are only a few drugs that give the proper therapeutic action. People who regularly take tranquilizers, antidepressants, and pain medication can often experience the following side effects: depression, anxiety, headaches, loss of appetite, phobias, stiffness and soreness, sinus pain, confusion, diarrhea or constipation, dizziness, loss of reality, blurred vision, emotional outbursts, anger and rage, slurred speech, lack of coordination, muscle spasms, memory impairment, personality changes, sore or achy joints, and emotional exhaustion.[1]

Withdrawal symptoms can range in severity and intensity from mild anxiety, irritability, and craving for the addicting substance to blackouts and seizures, although the latter are rare. Successfully coping with withdrawal and breaking addiction depends on:

1. General Health and age. Younger people commonly have "newer" habits. In addition, they are more resilient and generally have more physical resources to draw on.
2. Psychological stress load and mental state. Prerequisites for any successful withdrawal are a positive attitude and freedom from tension.
3. Length of time of addiction. Generally, the shorter the addiction, the easier it is to break.
4. Nature of the substance to which an individual is addicted.
5. Dosage or concentration of the addicted substance or medication, the spacing of dosages and route of administration.
6. Availability and extent of medical care, support groups, and family assistance, if needed, that can be expected.
7. Whether the addiction is part of a peer group milieu. Often these "friends" can contribute to the problem by peer pressure and the addict's need to fit in.
8. Personal habits, including the use of other drugs, medications, or alcohol. In order to have an effective recovery, the amount of chemicals in the body must be reduced.[2]

Recovery Time

The supreme hurdle most people face when detoxing from habit-forming substances is getting through the withdrawal uninjured despite its variety of physiological and emotional symptoms.[3] Do not become impatient, for it will take the body time to clean itself out of all the chemicals, toxins, and poisons to return to a normal state.

In recovery, the benzodiazepines and tranquilizers take the biggest toll on your brain and body. They cause physical dependence as well as psychological dependence—more even than do alcohol, cocaine, or heroin.

The number one question for those going into recovery is, "How long will it take before I am free?" Each person is biochemically unique, so the answer depends on your own biological make-up and the condition of your immune system. For some, recovery could take only weeks, others months, but with some it could be a year or more before all of the adverse symptoms are completely gone. Symptoms in the later months will not be as severe as in the beginning, but there are some nagging effects that linger.

At first, coping with stressful situations may not be easy after withdrawal is begun. Stress and anxiety at the time will be eased by the use of amino acids such as GABA, tryptophan, tyrosine, glutamine, lysine, methionine, vitamin B6 (pyrixodine), and niacinamide. The immune system must be restored and constant positive reinforcement given by a therapist.

Freedom from Pills

After taking tranquilizers, pain pills, or antidepressants for a long period, an individual can experience some or all of the following symptoms:

1. Increased anxiety attacks
2. Panic attacks
3. Depression
4. Personality changes
5. Skin and hair problems
6. Glazed eyes
7. Memory problems
8. Digestive upsets
9. Headaches
10. Constant pain
11. Sleep disorders
12. Weight loss or gain
13. Slow reaction time
14. No interest in sex

When a person has a chemical dependency, they cannot just stop. A steady reduction plan must be followed, along with a complete amino acid and nutrient therapy program, as well as a counseling program. This kind of treatment screens the body and brain from feeling severe symptoms, such as sudden drops in the level of the drug in the bloodstream.

The chronic abuse of psychoactive drugs usually leads to what has been termed psychological or psychic dependence. Your attitude and the intensity of your habit, how often you need and use a particular substance, such as tranquilizers or antidepressants, are all aspects which need analysis to aid in your recovery. Those with chronic abuse syndrome have not only psychological dependence but also an obsession which affects their emotional makeup, mind, and lifestyle.

Guilt should never influence recovery; if you have had an anxiety or depression problem and were given these medications by a physician, you were following what you thought was a therapeutic dose. However, <u>when a drug has been taken continuously for more than 4 to 6 months, it has little therapeutic effect on the original symptoms.</u> The user may only be avoiding withdrawal symptoms by continuing the medication, and he still suffers the toxic effects of the drug.

Just as guilt is a significant factor, so is fear. Constant reinforcement is needed so that fear does not impede recovery. Behavior therapists are of great assistance in substance abuse. They give constant reassurance to aid you in succeeding. Weekly sessions are the best, if possible. A physician should be consulted regarding a detox program; if he sees a problem, specific instructions should be given to the patient to prepare him. Careful attention should be given to the complete withdrawal of such drugs from an elderly dependent person, and it should be done only under the supervision of a physician.

The speed at which withdrawal from any substance is practical depends on what is happening in your life. If you have to operate machinery, drive, have small children, have a stressful job or have a sick person dependent on you, then withdrawal must be done slowly.

WITHDRAWAL TABLE

Benziodiazepines—Valium (Diazepam 18 mg (2 mg tablets)

Week	Morning	Lunch	Evening	Total	Mg Total
1	2.5 tabs	2.5 tabs	2.5 tabs	= 7.5 tabs	15 mg
2	2.0 tabs	2.0 tabs	2.0 tabs	= 6.0 tabs	12 mg
3	1.5 tabs	1.5 tabs	1.5 tabs	= 4.5 tabs	9 mg
4	1.0 tab	1.0 tab	1.0 tab	= 3.0 tabs	6 mg
5	.5 tab	.5 tab	.5 tab	= 1.5 tabs	3 mg

THIS SCHEDULE CAN BE USED FOR WITHDRAWAL FROM MOST OF THE BENZIODIAZEPINES.
REDUCE ONLY ¼TH OF THE DAILY DOSAGE PER 7 DAYS!

Reduction Procedures

Some doctors may recommend hospitalization for withdrawal following a planned program, but many people achieve withdrawal very well at home. If a physician agrees reduction should take place, but fails to recommend a detox schedule, the drug detoxification handbooks used in most psychiatric hospitals recommend a dose reduction of **¼th the daily dose per 7 days.** (Never compare the number of milligrams; 1 mg of one drug cannot be substituted for 1 mg of another drug. For example, 5 mg of Valium does not equal 5 mg of Halcion or 5 mg of Ativan.)

The body and brain cry and scream wildly at the anticipation of a reduction or not receiving the drugs or substance they are accustomed to receiving. Considering what drugs are supposed to do—for example, relax muscles, control anxiety, or aid sleep—it is understandable that the body and mind object after they have become accustomed to having it present. The rebound reaction, i.e., the opposite of the desired effect, occurs in many people, at least for a period of withdrawal. In the following list of withdrawal symptoms, note that some people may only experience a few of them, especially if they withdraw slowly.

Withdrawal Symptoms by Addictive Substance

Medications: Weight loss, chills, hiccups, low back pain, (For Anxiety, muscle twitching, muscle weakness, tremors, Depression, weakness, apathy, craving for the medication/ Pain, Sleep, substance, delirium, depression, dizziness, Hyperactivity, fatigue, insomnia, irritability, loss of appetite, Phobias, nightmares, panic, anger, rage, crawling and Fear) sensations on skin, seizures, gooseflesh, rashes, incontinence, stomachaches, intestinal cramps, nausea and vomiting, diarrhea, constipation, yawning, bad taste in mouth, aching in ears, runny nose, smelling of unpleasant odors, watery eyes, uncontrolled blinking, rapid movement of the eyes, dilated pupils, double vision, headaches, muscle contraction headaches, increased anxiety, panic or anxiety attacks, agoraphobia, flu-like symptoms, hyperactivity, hallucinations, confusion, sweating, palpitations, slow or rapid pulse, tight chest, abdominal pain, restlessness, increased sensitivity to noise, light, touch, or smell, change in sex interest, impotence, pains in the shoulder, neck, jaw, or face, jitteriness, and shaking.

Cocaine: Irritability, runny nose, nasal tissue irritation, weight loss or gain, muscle aches, muscle twitching, muscular weakness, anxiety, apathy, craving for cocaine, delirium, depression, fatigue, paranoia, hallucinations, inability to concentrate, insomnia, hyperactivity, nightmares.

Alcohol: Anxiety, craving for addictive substance, delerium, depression, dizziness, fatigue, hallucinations, loss of appetite, hyperactivity, inability to concentrate, insomnia, temporary insanity, tension, unsteady gait, chills, dehydration, fever and sweating, muscle weakness, tremors, weakness, dilated pupils, rapid side-to-side movement of eyeballs, dry mouth, nausea, and vomiting.

Caffeine: Irritability, muscle contraction headaches, migraine headaches, runny nose, tinnitus (ringing in the ears), rapid pulse, diarrhea, flushing, stomachaches, cramps, urinary frequency, flushing, apathy, craving for coffee, delirium, depression, drowsiness, inability to concentrate, tension, unsteady gait, chills, fever and sweating, tremors, weakness.

Marijuana: Anxiety, hyperactivity, loss of appetite, craving for marijuana, delerium, depression, drowsiness, insomnia, irritability.

Nicotine: Weight gain, muscle aches, craving for cigarettes/nicotine, delerium, depression, drowsiness, irritability, insomnia, diarrhea, sore gums or tongue, constipation, stomachaches, intestional cramping, muscle contraction headaches.

Sugar: Anxiety, craving for sugar, delerium, rage, depression, dizziness, hyperactivity, inability to concentrate, irritability, anger, tremors, weakness, muscle contraction headaches, blurred vision, rapid heartbeat.[4]

Heroin: Anxiety, runny nose, dilated pupils, irritability, disturbed sleep, cramps, diarrhea, vomiting, shaking chills, profuse sweating, sleep disturbances, aches and pains.

Barbiturates: Anxiety, sleep disturbances, irritability, restlessness, postural hypotension, delirium, major motor seizures, fever.[5]

All withdrawal symptoms pass in time. Knowledge and acceptance of the withdrawal symptoms can shorten the recovery time. The goal of physical and mental well-being represents a state that an addicted person may not have experienced for many years.

Anxiety

The majority of withdrawal symptoms are due to manifestations of anxiety. This does not mean simply worrying about the weather, but disabling physical and emotional symptoms which prevent the sufferer from leading a normal life. Studies have verified that anxiety levels after drugs have been stopped can be six times greater than pre-withdrawal levels; this is known as rebound anxiety.[6]

Tranquilizers make those who are taking them feel as though that part of the brain that deals with anxiety has stopped functioning properly, but it does function at an accelerated rate day and night. The feeling of acceleration is a temporary sensation, and with time it passes.

Drugs may act by stimulating or depressing the normal physiological function of specific organs. Stimulation is an increase in the rate of functional activity of a cell or in the amount of secretion from a gland. Depression denotes a reduction in such activity. Amphetamine and caffeine stimulate the central nervous system, whereas alcohol and phenobarbital depress the brain.

Drugs cannot endow a tissue or cell with properties they do not inherently possess. Thus, no drug is capable of stimulating the epithelial cell located in the mouth to release insulin. A drug cannot transform a muscle fiber in such a manner that it functions as a nerve cell. Drugs can stimulate or depress the normal activity of a nerve or muscle cell. In addition, stimulants such as amphetamines possess a biphasic activity...that is, in moderate doses amphetamines cause stimulatoin, but at higher doses they cause depression. Drugs are unable to restore diseased organs or tissue functions to normal by a direct action.[7]

Neurotransmitters are the chemical language of the brain. These neurotransmitters and endorphins must be produced by the brain for normal functioning during withdrawal.[8] It takes time for the brain's receptor sites to be restored to their normal pattern. Knowledge is power: you need to understand these processes and know that the capability is there to control anxious messages, stress, and depression, and give the brain time to recover.[9]

Grief Reactions

Those going through bereavement are often offered

tranquilizers, "to help you get through the tough time." Not only do you run the risk of dependence, but because the drug dulls the emotions you are unable to adjust to the loss or altered situation.[10] You have to face the grief again when the medication ceases, and you may even feel severe guilt about not facing your loss, not having been able to say goodbye or grieve at the "proper" time. In later years, suppressed emotions can come to the surface and cause withdrawal, depression, and delayed grief. As suppressed emotions are released, old fears, phobias, guilts, and anxiety are resolved, and self-respect is regained. It is then that most people are finally able to face old conflicts, traumas, and unresolved anxieties.

Stress Reactions

The key to controlling stress reaction is to conquer the stressors which cause the limbic system in the brain to fire constant messages at the cortex, the reasoning part of the brain. During stress and physical illness, this mechanism may become over-stimulated, and the constant anxiety causes an imbalance in the brain's chemistry. Feelings that accompany stress are rapid heart beat, churning stomach, shaking, sweating, feeling of unreality, blurred vision, fear of not being able to get help in time, and fear of death.

The number one stressor in the world today is <u>uncertainty,</u> and drugs cannot solve this problem for you. Uncertainty comes when we feel a loss of control in our lives. Post-traumatic stress is often a major factor—we are playing old tapes of painful events in our past; we are fearful of the future, and still enduring grief over events in the past. With help we can put a face on the fear, let time pass, and use relaxation/deep breathing, amino acids, and nutrients to restore an oversensitized nervous system, brain, and body.

Many withdrawal symptoms are due to rebound anxiety according to the *Oxford Textbook of Psychiatry.*

Anxiety neuroses have both physical and psychological symptoms. The psychological symptoms include fearful anticipation, irritability, difficulty in concentrating, sensitivity to noise, and a feeling of restlessness. Patients often complain of poor memory, probably due to lack of concentration.

Repetitious thoughts make up an important part of anxiety neurosis. These are often provoked by awareness of the automatic over-activity; for example, a patient feels his heart beating fast or pounding in his chest and may fear a heart attack. Thoughts of this kind will probably prolong the condition.

The appearance of someone with anxiety neurosis is distinctive. His face appears strained, with a furrowed brow; he is restless and frequently shaky; his posture is tense, his skin looks pale, and often he will sweat from his hands, feet, and armpits. There is also increased tension in the skeletal muscles or over-stimulation of the sympathetic nervous system.

The list of symptoms is extensive and is grouped according to systems in the body.

Symptoms related to the gastrointestinal system include rumbling of intestinal gases, frequent or loose bowel movements, excessive air swallowing, epigastric pain (under sternum or breastbone), dry mouth, and feelings of "butterflies" in the stomach.

Cardiovascular symptoms include palpitations, an awareness of missed or irregular heartbeats, throbbing in the neck, feeling of discomfort or pain over the heart or chest, increased or rapid pulse.

Common respiratory symptoms include hyperventilation, a feeling of constriction in the chest, and difficulty in catching the breath.

Genitourinary symptoms are increased frequency and urgency of urination, failure of erection, and lack of sexual interest. Women may complain of increased menstrual discomfort or difficulty, and sometimes absence of menstruation.

Other complaints related to the functions of the

central nervous system including ringing in the ears, dizziness, prickling sensations, blurred vision, muscular tension in back and shoulders; sleep disturbances such as insomnia, then intermittent awakening, and unpleasant dreams; depersonalization, not feeling in touch with reality, lack of concentration, memory loss, and panic attacks.[11]

VITAMINS AND NUTRIENTS THAT AID IN RECOVERY FROM DRUGS

Nutrient	Usage	Therapeutic Dosage
Vitamin E	Detoxification, antioxidant	Start with 400 I.U. then increase to 800 I.U. after two weeks and continue daily
Esterified C	Detoxes, anti-free radicals	2-5 gm /day
B Complex	Important in nervous system. Important cofactor in many body reactions.	100 mg twice /day
Magnesium	Mental Function	500-1000 mg
Beta Carotene	Detoxification, antioxident	10,000 I.U. daily
Multiple Vitamin	Replenish body	If tablet, break in half, take ½ in AM and ½ in PM
GABA 750	Any anxiety	Dissolved in water 2 to 3 times daily, spread out, must be pure GABA
Tyrosine	Depression	850-1000 mg 2 to 3 times daily, spread out
Ginseng	Adaptagen. Increases body's resistance to stress	500-1000 mg daily AM & PM

Medication Withdrawal Procedure

It is important to learn all that you can about any drug you are taking. Check with your pharmacist, physician, check the *Physician's Desk Reference* or other reference books on the medication or drugs. **Ask questions. DO NOT be intimidated.**

You can begin by gathering the following information:

1. Determine how addictive the drug is.
2. Determine if YOU are addicted. You are if:
   a) Missing even one dosage makes you feel sick, nervous, sad, or you experience a craving for the drug.
   b) You need the drug to function normally.
   c) You begin to require a larger dosage to obtain the same effect.
   d) You continue to use the drug in spite of side effects or other negative reactions.
   e) There is a family history of alcohol or substance abuse.
3. Observe in yourself the withdrawal effects for rapid and slow withdrawal.
4. How long do the withdrawal syptoms last?
5. Can these withdrawal symptoms be minimized without using other medications?

Never stop using a prescription medication unless you have strong feelings and reasons to believe it is harmful to you. Some physicians may not understand your reason for stopping the medication and may feel that you are trying to be an uncooperative patient. They might not support your need to stop and will reassure you that the drug is safe for you whatever duration you want to take it. But remember that it is your body, and the prescription may not always be in your best interest. Don't hesitate to get a second or third opinion from doctors of different orientations and then make your decision based on this information. Drug therapy is a valid medical procedure, but for the most part it is a temporary measure, and to be used only when there is no alternative.

If you decide to quit the drug, know what the withdrawal syptoms are *before* withdrawing. Determine your method and schedule of withdrawal with a physician if possible. If your dependency is minor, it probably can be done at home. If your dependency is major, you will probably need to be in a medical facility for close medical supervision. Be aware that many facilities and physicians use other drugs to withdraw from different substances. The worst possible treatment is substituting one drug or chemical for another.

Once your withdrawal effects have been overcome, the next step is to remain off the offending drug or substance. Explore amino acid therapy, and add biofeedback, meditation, homeopathic formulas, phenolics (the neutralization of toxic reactions), herbology (the study and application of herbs), and acupuncture to remain free of the substance. Form new habits and friends by joining Alcoholics Anonymous or Narcotics Anonymous or Palmer Group; these are great support groups and all of the members have had a problem at one time or another. Take one day at a time. Keep alert; become an informed educated consumer; know what you are putting into your body. Ask questions. Do not take any medication unless you know why it is being given to you and what it will do in your body and mind.

Esterified C

Vitamin C is most important in the treatment of anxiety, stress, depression, and pain. In 1987, clinical studies established that Ester C Polyascorbate is totally neutral, having a pH of 7.0. It does not cause gastrointestinal upsets or diarrhea. It is proven four times more bioavailable than ordinary vitamin C.

Esterified C is a unique complex mixture with a distinctive molecular personality. This means that this form of vitamin C is most available to the tissues of the body, and is available within 20 minutes after ingestion, and 24 hours later some of it is still there. Ordinary vitamin C is out of the body within 4 hours after ingestion; even time-release vitamin C has been excreted while the esterified vitamin C is still working and available to the body.

All humans, adults, and children need vitamin C, and they need it daily. Esterified C has been extremely effective in our detoxification program. At the Pain & Stress Therapy Center, we use varying doses for adults in detoxification ranging from 2 to 10,000 mg daily.

Allergic Reactions

Doris J. Rapp, M.D., Pediatric and Family Allergist, who treats many hyperactive children, in her books *Allergies and the Hyperactive Child* and *Allergies and Your Family*, outlines medical symptoms which are due to allergic reactions—not because there are emotional problems. Dr. Rapp refers to this as the "allergic-tension-fatigue syndrome." The medical symptoms include:

Nose: year-round stuffiness, watery nose, sneezing, nose-rubbing.

Aches: head, back, neck, muscles, joints, growing pains, or aches unrelated to exercise.

Belly problems: bellyaches, nausea, upset stomach, bloating, bad breath, gas stomach, belching, vomiting, diarrhea, constipation.

Bladder problems: wetting pants in the daytime or in bed, need to rush to urinate, burning or pain with urination.

Face: pale, dark eye circles, puffiness below eyes.

Glands: swelling of lymph nodes of neck.

Ear problems: repeated formation of fluid behind eardrums, ringing ears, dizziness, excessive perspiration, and low grade fever.

Dr. Rapp states some children as well as adults are tired, weak, mentally confused, ittitable, drowsy, depressed, have body aches, fever, chills, and night sweats. They often sleep poorly, awaken at night, have nightmares, and cry out in their sleep. And they often have learning problems.

In *Allergies and Your Family*, Dr. Rapp, one of the country's foremost family allergists, describes causes, symptoms, cures, and the eventual prevention of many allergies. Approximately one million children are currently taking Ritalin for hyperactivity that could be caused by allergic responses to food and chemicals or a poor diet.

From available information, there are millions of adults who are taking some type of tranquilizer, anti-depressant, or powerful stimulant, never aware their symptoms could be caused by allergic reactions to food or chemicals.

We highly recommend Dr. Rapp's books for the whole family.

SOME MENTAL SYMPTOMS RELATED TO FOOD ALLERGY

Aggression	Fearful	Paranoia
Agitation	Feelings of unreality	Psychoses
Anxiety	Hallucinations	Pugnaciousness
Compulsions	"High-strung"	Quarrelsomeness
Concentration, lack of	Hysteria	Rage
Confusion	Impatience	Restlessness
Consider suicide	Insomnia	Screaming
Crying easily	Irresponsibility	Sensitiveness
Cruelty	Irritability	Slow thought processes
Delirium	Jumpiness	Stupor
Delusion	Lethargy	Talkativeness
Depression	Loss of interest in life	Temper
Difficult to please	Mania	Tenseness
Disorientation	Meanness	Uncooperativeness
Distraction	Mental confusion	Unhappiness
Dreaminess	Morbidness	Unpredictableness
Drowsiness	Nervousness	Unreasonableness
Easily hurt	Neuroses	Whining
Erratic	Nightmares	Worries
Excitability	Panic	

III
Alcoholism and
its Treatment

There are over 100 million people in the United States who drink alcohol. Of these, over 10 million are alcoholics. Alcoholism is ranked the number two killer in this country behind cancer. Many experts believe alcoholism actually outranks cancer as our number one killer, since alcoholism is commonly the "undiagnosed" cause of listed "Cause of Death." The cost to the economy approaches $50 billion every year![1]

While there is no one "personality" of an alcoholic, in 1974 Doctors Hague and Howard reported that alcoholics reacted to stress differently than did a nondrinker control group. Changes in eating and sleeping habits and changes in vacations and holidays, divorce, a death in the family, or a job loss caused the alcoholic to feel more stress than a nonalcoholic.[2] Specific personality traits may become more prominent or result in bizarre transformations. The introvert may become extroverted, the gentle one violent, the sensitive one insensitive, and so on. In the early stages, an alcoholic is often irritable, very moody, and depressed when he is not imbibing. He denies that he is drinking too much, blaming his drinking on his wife, his job, stress, etc.[3]

An alcoholic sees the world around him as close,

threatening, and anxiety-producing. The alcoholic uses alcohol to solve his problems because these scary feelings disappear after a drink—his blood alcohol increases and the self-degenerating circuits of the brain are anesthetized.. The alcohol is a way of acknowledging or dealing with depression as it gives a temporary lift and relief from the depression, but the relief is short-lived because alcohol is a central nervous system depressant. After the high wears off the depression may intensify. So the addiction goes on and on.[4]

PROGRESSION OF DRINKING SYMPTOMS

Development Stage	Social drinking Once a week Drinking faster than associates Drinking more than associates Blackouts (memory) More drunk than associates Avoidance of family closeness
Overt Alcoholism	Loss of control Before breakfast Protects supply Weekends lost Solitary drinking Will not share thinking or ideas Wants to escape Tremors Decreased tolerance
Deterioration Stage	Vague fears Prefers solitary life Delirium tremors Insomnia Loss or depletion of vitamin stores Death[5]

Alcohol shares many similar properties with the hypnotic

and anti-anxiety drugs.[6] Alcohol seems to serve as courage for the alcoholic since it works primarily on anticipatory anxiety. The alcoholic is in a state of chronic anxiety. As a side note, alcohol has been shown to operate as an MAO inhibitor, which is a category of anti-depressant.[7]

SYMPTOMS OF ALCOHOL WITHDRAWAL (MILD OR EARLY)

Behavior Changes
> Irritability
> Restlessness
> Agitation
> Hostility
> Exaggerated startle response

Sleep Disturbances
> Insomnia
> Restless sleep
> Nightmares

Impaired Cognitive Function
> Easily distracted
> Impairment of memory
> Inability to concentrate
> Impairment of judgement and other mental functions

Muscular Symptoms
> Cramps
> Weakness
> Trembling

Gastrointestinal Problems
> Appetite loss
> Nausea
> Vomiting
> Abdominal discomfort
> Diarrhea

Autonomic Imbalances
> Tachycardia or rapid heart beat greater than 100 beats/minute

Systolic hypertension (high blood pressure)
Shakiness
Fever
Sweating or diaphoresis

SYMPTOMS OF ALCOHOL WITHDRAWAL
(LATE OR SEVERE)

Worsening of mild symptoms of alcohol withdrawal
Tremor
Tachycardia
Agitation
Diaphoresis
Marked startle response
Delusions
Paranoia
Mixed with and reinforced by hallucinations
Can create agitation and terror
Delirium
Changes from one hour to the next in
severity and nature
Impairment of thinking
Disorientation as to time and place
Clouding of senses
Hallucinations
Can be visual, auditory, or tactile
Can be threatening in nature
Seizures
Usually generalized and nonfocal
History of prior seizure disorder not
necessary
Usually occurs within 48 hours after
cessation of drinking
Usually self-limiting
Always precede severe delirium, agitation,
and hallucinations[8]

All mammals, including humans, make a small
amount of alcohol in the body as part of normal metab-

olism. In this process the average person makes about one ounce of alcohol per day, which is broken down in the liver by an enzyme called alcohol dehydrogenase. This enzyme also handles the alcohol ingested from alcoholic beverages.

In the next step, alcohol is converted by alcohol dehydrogenase to acetaldehyde, and this substance can damage the body in several ways:

1. It can cause abnormal chemical bonds in large molecules like proteins (causing hardening of the arteries, loss of elasticity, skin wrinkling).
2. It can damage the DNA molecule (resulting in abnormal cell function.
3. Damage can also result when acetaldehyde is oxidized in the body, yielding dangerous and reactive chemical fragments called free radicals; these can cause damage to many cell structures, cancer, birth defects, atherosclerosis, and are implicated as major factors in aging.

****

METABOLISM OF ALCOHOL

Alcohol---------- ► alcohol dehydrogenase---- ► acetaldehyde

Acetaldehyde --- ► aldehydrogenase ----------- ► acetate
(common vinegar)

Acetate----------- ► carbon dioxide + water

****

Acetaldehyde is a very toxic chemical, and the body breaks it down by the enzyme called aldehyde dehydrogenase; this is a most crucial breakdown. If the liver does not produce enough aldehyde dehydrogenase many toxic side effects can occur, especially to the liver cells. "Normal" people who do not ingest excess alcohol have no difficulty breaking down the alcohol to acetate in their bodies. The enzyme system can be overloaded when alcohol is ingested too quickly. Acetaldehyde and its free radical by-products from the alcohol breakdown cause most of the damage to the body and the brain, including cardiovascular disease, premature aging, liver damage, brain damage, lowered resistance to disease, alcohol addiction, etc.

In the brain an overload of acetaldehyde can lead to bizarre and complicated chemical reactions. It competes with other chemical substances known as brain amines or neurotransmitters for the attention of certain enzymes. Acetaldehyde blocks the enzymes from achieving their primary duty of inhibiting the neurotransmitter activity. Addiction to alcohol might never occur if acetaldehyde stopped interfering at this point with the brain's chemical activities. The brain neurotransmitters interact with acetaldehyde to form compounds called isoquinolines. These compounds also release the stored neurotransmitters. The isoquinolines are very similar to the opiates, and research has suggested that they may act on the opiate receptors in the brain. The opiate receptors may contribute to the addiction of alcohol. These mischievous substances may trigger the alcoholic to drink more and more to counter the painful effects of the increasing buildup of acetaldehyde.[9]

Recently scientists have discovered that many alcoholics have a metabolic defect which causes them to have twice as much of the toxic acetaldehyde in their bloodstreams after a drink as normal people. This is enough to set the vicious cycle into motion. Acetaldehyde made by the liver makes the drinker feel bad so he drinks more alcohol; this makes him feel better and helps to protect him from the acetaldehyde poison— until the liver produces more acetaldehyde out of the additional alcohol, so he indulges and has some more drinks, and on and on goes the cycle.

Researchers have looked and continue to look for the one cause of alcoholism. But all research has concluded that there is no one factor; studies have shown that a number of physiological differences exist between the nonalcoholic and the alcoholic. Physiology determines whether one person becomes alcoholic and another does not. The alcoholic's body—his hormones, enzymes, genes, and brain chemistry—all work jointly to cause his abnormal reaction to alcohol. Of course, psychological, family history, and social factors certainly influence the alcoholic's drinking habits and behavior.[10]

Alcoholism and nutrition are interrelated and intertwined on many levels:
1. Ethyl alcohol, or ethanol, itself contains nutrients; however, it also changes the balance of other nutrients in the diet and may disperse them as well.
2. The absorption and digestion of many nutrients is affected by the ingestion of ethanol; it may alter dietary requirements.
3. In addiction, nutritional alterations may affect the metabolism of alcohol in the body.
4. Chronic alcohol consumption may cause temporary or permanent damage to many organs—the liver, brain, heart, and bone marrow. The effects may be modified by nutritional factors such as dietary intake of protein, fat, and vitamins.
5. Organ damage may yield changes in nutrient metabolism. The organ most affected is the liver. The liver plays an important role in metabolism and is frequently altered with alcohol ingestion.[11]

Identifying the cause of malnutrition in alcoholism is not a simple matter. Certain groups of alcoholics may have an inadequate nutrient intake, but a major factor is the primary toxic effect of ethanol on the gastrointestinal tract, pancreas, liver, bone marrow, and other tissues such as the heart. Research data by Rubin and Lieber in 1974 suggested that a nutritious diet could not and will not prevent the development of alcoholic liver disease.[12]

FACTORS LEADING TO MALNUTRITION IN ALCOHOLISM

1. Decreased or sporadic food ingestion
   Intoxication
   Poverty and economic factors
   Abnormal appetite
   Anorexia
   Mental illness/disease

2. Increased nutrient losses
   Urinary
   Toxic effects of alcohol on the kidneys
   Fecal
     a) Malabsorption due to GI effects of alcohol
     b) Maldigestion due to inflamed pancreas

3. Reduced or deficient nutrient stores
   Decreased uptake of nutrients
   Alcoholic hepatitis
   Cirrhosis (inflammation of liver)
   Reduced nutrient intake
   Increased inactivation of vitamins and nutrients

4. Impaired nutrient utilization due to defective metabolism
   Alcoholic liver disease
   Toxic effects of alcohol on bone marrow.[13]

Alcoholic beverages provide mainly calories which are derived from their ethanol content. A pint of 86 proof liquor supplies about half the normal daily calories required by an adult, but these alcoholic calories are utterly empty of other nutrients.[14] Ethanol does not even provide caloric food value equal to carbohydrates.[15] If alcohol consumption is heavy and the drinker limits his food intake, he worsens his already severe vitamin and nutrient deficiencies. Conversely, if he does not reduce his food intake, many of the extra ethanol calories are converted to fat, causing high serum triglyceride levels and obesity. Niacin or vitamin B3 has been used to lower these serum lipids (fats) by 25% within two weeks.[16] There is now a product combining niacin with guar gum that is unique because the niacin does not cause flushing. (Flushing is a common side effect of niacin.)

Acute and chronic consumption of alcohol may markedly alter digestion and gastrointestinal absorption. Alcohol-induced changes in digestion and absorption may yield marginal deficiencies arising from other causes.[17]

A number of neurological syndromes occurring with the chronic usage of alcohol are attributed to vitamin deficiencies. Just to name a few, these include: Wernicke's disease, Korsakoff's syndrome, peripheral neuropathy, Morel's corticoid sclerosis, and cellular degeneration. Alterations in the metabolism of the B vitamins in the alcoholic person affect the levels in his body. Commonly, the level of B1 (thiamine), B3 (niacin), B6 (pyridoxine), B12, B15, and folic acid are decreased in the alcoholic. Anemias are seen with deficiencies of folic acid or B6 while deficiencies of niacin or thiamine may cause neurological syndromes.

ALCOHOL/DRUG-INDUCED NUTRITIONAL DEFICIENCIES

Vitamins Depleted	Minerals Depleted	Protein Depleted
Folic acid	Magnesium	
Thiamine	Zinc	
Riboflavin		
Niacin		
Ascorbic acid		
Vitamin B6		
Vitamin B12[18]		

The metabolism of the fat-soluble vitamins may be altered due to the alcohol ingestion. In alcoholics with cirrhosis, Vitamin A deficiencies may occur; this is due to malabsorption, impaired liver storage of vitamin A, or simply too much alcohol in the body competing in the liver. Vitamin D may be depleted through dietary insufficiency. Vitamin K deficiency in the alcoholic may manifest itself as a bleeding disorder related to the liver's failure to make clotting factors.

Mineral deficiencies can be caused by alcohol, especially magnesium and zinc; alcohol increases the excretion of magnesium and zinc via the kidneys. Magnesium depletion can be responsible for the symptoms of the "horror" or delirium tremors. Low levels of calcium have been found due to increased excretion of calcium in the urine over a period of years; this can lead to osteoporosis.

The excessive intake of alcohol is one factor which precipitates clinical vitamin deficiencies. This depletion usually includes many of the vitamins, but the most common are: folic acid, thiamine, riboflavin, niacin, B6, B12, and vitamin C. Mineral depletion usually includes magnesium and zinc. A protein deficiency usually exists due to malnutrition. The alcoholic has a wide range of deficiencies and needs nutritional supplementation.[19]

Treatment

Treatment for and control of the ingestion of alcohol requires a team effort. Good nutrition can help in the control by maintaining an adequate blood sugar level. Dr. Robert Meiers has found a low blood sugar level (hypoglycemia) in 95% of alcoholics; this results from the lack of food intake and substituting alcohol for essential calories and nutrients.[20] Hypoglycemia has been implicated as one of the contributing factors in the cause of alcoholism. If the blood sugar drops, the alcoholic needs a drink.[21]

Abstinence is the ultimate goal. The greatest majority of alcoholics cannot become social drinkers again because they tend to relapse into heavy drinking. In *Feed Yourself Right* by Lendon Smith, M.D., he states, "All people who drink must remember that alcohol is a biochemical stress, and each swallow must be accompanied with B vitamins, some nourishing food, and at least sometime that day or week, the minerals known to be lost must be replaced."

Nutrient and Amino Acid Program for the Therapeutic Treatment of Alcoholism

Please note the following supplements should be taken on a daily basis to maintain brain chemistry and control craving.

B Complex 200 mg	½ tablet in the AM and ½ in the PM
Calcium 1,000 mg **Magnesium 500 mg** **and Zinc 30 mg**	2-3 at bedtime
Esterified C **2-3,000 mg daily**	Half in the AM and half in PM
DLPA + Glutamine **500 mg + 500 mg with** **Niacinamide 50 mg and** **Pyridoxine (B6) 5 mg**	1-2 caplets with each meal
Tyrosine + GABA **Combination, A Stress/** **Anxiety Formula** (Patent-Pending Formula)	1-2 with each meal
Tryptophan 500 mg (Note: We use Trypto + GABA combination to keep down craving of alcohol and the serotonin level in the brain high.	2 an hour before bedtime with fruit or fruit juice
Good Multiple Vitamin	1 every AM to give you other needed nutrients

The patient will notice a difference in the way he feels after 1 week on this regimen. After 6 months, if control is maintained then the maintenance dose would be:

B Complex	½ in AM and ½ in PM
Good Multiple Vitamin	1 in AM
DLPA + Glutamine	1 with each meal
Stress/Anxiety Formula	1 with each meal
Tryptophan	2 an hour before bedtime

This same program is used for cocaine and other recreational drugs in the same dosages and time frames. If needed, Phase I can be used as long as necessary.

We would like to mention here, and strongly recommend that if you have an alcohol or substance abuse problem, you seek out a psychotherapist or behavior therapist that you can work with and get counseling for yourself and your family. If you are the child of an alcoholic you are predisposed to an addictive personality and should seek counseling.

IV
Nicotine and Caffeine Addiction and Treatment

Although the number of smokers in the United States has decreased, approximately one-fourth of the population continues to smoke or use nicotine in some form. Nicotine is an oily poisonous liquid found only in the tobacco plant. Pharmaceutically, it is characterized as an organic nerve drug; it is so powerful that one drop injected in a human can cause instant death.[1]

Four types of smoking dependency have been identified by Karl-Olov Fagerstrom of Sweden:

Type 1 is the social smoker. He smokes for image, using it as a way of relieving tension and to give him something to do with his hands.

Type 2 is the person whose smoking habit evolves around daily activities such as breaks, meals, telephone calls, etc, as well as social functions.

Type 3 is one who is chemically or emotionally dependent on nicotine; he is "hooked" on it. This person smokes all day long, from just awakening until bedtime. A certain plasma level of nicotine must be maintained or he will experience withdrawal symptoms.

Type 4 has a psychological and chemical dependency. He smokes more heavily and inhales more deeply than Type 3.[2]

Tobacco smoking depletes the body of Vitamins A, B1, (Thiamine), B5 (Pantothenic Acid), B6 (Pyridoxine), C, and E. The amino acid cysteine is also depleted. Every cigarette burns about 25 mg of Vitamin C—possibly one of the reasons smokers generally look older than their non-smoking counterpart. These deficiencies may contribute to mood swings and possibly depression.[3]

Nicotine readily crosses the blood-brain barrier. It is distributed throughout the brain, and its uptake appears to involve both passive diffusion and active transport. Within the brain, the specific binding of nicotine is greatest in the hypothalmus, hippocampus, thalamus, midbrain, and brain stem, as well as in areas of the cerebral cortex. Short-term exposure to nicotine results in the activation of several central nervous system neurohormonal pathways resulting in the release of acetylcholine, norepinephrine, dopamine, serotonin, vasopressin, growth hormone, and ACTH.

Most of the effects of nicotine on the central nervous system are due to direct actions on brain receptors. Nicotine causes the release of catecholamines and facilitates the release of neurotransmitters from sympathetic nerves in blood vessels. Stimulation of the sympathetic nervous system results in an increased heart rate and blood pressure while the blood flow to the extremities decreases due to constriction of blood vessels.

Nicotine freely crosses the placenta and has been found in amniotic fluid and umbilical cord blood in newborns. Additionally, it is found in breast milk.[4]

Nicotine Withdrawal Program

Make a decision that you are going to quit. Today you have become a non-smoker. Put your heart into the decision, and mean it 100%. Decide whether to quit slowly or rapidly. There are advantages to both, so you must decide what is best for you. Some people like to slowly taper down on their cigarette/nicotine habit; others find quitting "cold turkey" is the best way to handle the habit. When you taper down, the nicotine commonly causes a craving in the brain for more. It is as though you have a full tank and when your gas tank (your brain and body) starts noticing a decrease in the level of nicotine your body wants to replenish that level to full, so you crave nicotine.

If you decide to quit slowly, set a target date a month in advance. Ask your family and friends to reinforce your decision by supporting you. Invite a friend to also quit. Keep a journal of each day during the 4 weeks, noting the exact time of every cigarette that you smoke and why. Decrease usage. You might try delaying each cigarette that you smoke by 5 minutes the first day, 6 minutes the second, and so forth until you have quit. Change to a brand that you dislike. Change hands from the hand you normally use with a cigarette. Using aversion therapy such as imagining that the cigarettes taste like the smell of ashes or imagining that the cigarettes taste just as bad as the first time you put one to your mouth, works well for some people. On the day you quit, throw all your cigarettes away. Get rid of ashtrays, matches, etc.[5]

Conversely, if you quit quickly, or cold turkey, you may experience withdrawal symptoms, but many people find this is the best way. The nicotine is out of the system in 24 hours, but the craving may continue for 72 hours. Many people experience withdrawal symptoms such as irritability, depression, anxiety, headaches, and sleep disorders for the first 72 hours; after 3 days, the craving for nicotine is simply a habit of reaching for a cigarette/nicotine.

But once you stop, think only of yourself as a NON-smoker. If at any time you desire a cigarette, take in a very, very deep breath because your body is actually craving oxygen; this can stop the urge for a cigarette. Sit in the nonsmoking section of restaurants.

Many people fear gaining weight after they quit smoking. It is true your metabolism does slow down, only very slightly. You may experience your stomach growling or churning because it has been producing more hydrochloric acid to overcome the nicotine that was swallowed. Some peppermint in the form of tea, gum, or a candy may help quiet the stomach. Watching your diet and food consumption closely can help prevent a weight gain. It takes two to three months for your body to return to its regular metabolic rate after you quit smoking. As a cleaning process, your body flushes fluid into the tissues; this may reinforce the belief that you will gain weight when you quit smoking. It is only temporary, and drinking plenty of water and fluids will help.

The most common problem that smokers experience is what to do with their hands. Stay busy! Pick up a new hobby like exercising, walking, crocheting, knitting, whittling, or cleaning. Remember, it takes 21-25 days to form a new habit.

If you had a habit of smoking a cigarette after meals, change your habit by going for a short walk instead. But DO NOT try to also cut down or quit drinking coffee (caffeine) at the same time that you are stopping smoking. It will produce too much stress on your system if you experience both nicotine and caffeine withdrawal at the same time. Conquer the nicotine habit first, then the caffeine at a later date.

Probably the next most common problem is irritability, jitteriness, and reaching for a cigarette at the first sign of stress. The one leads to two and before you know it, you are back smoking.

We have successfully used a combination program at the Pain & Stress Therapy Center in San Antonio. We use the Stress and Anxiety Formula amino acids, GABA 750, Esterified Vitamin C, and nutrients which inhibit the craving for nicotine. Additionally, hypnosis is sometimes employed to assist quitting. Try to decrease your intake of meat, seafood, eggs, and poultry. Eat plenty of fruits and vegetables; these foods help to make your urine more alkaline and help you eliminate the nicotine from your system more quickly.

Caffeine

Probably one of the most used drugs in the world is caffeine. It is extremely popular because it is mentally stimulating. It is found in tea, coffee, soft drinks, some over the counter pain pills, and in the herb guarana. Recently, colas have replaced coffee as the number one source of caffeine intake.[6]

Caffeine belongs to one of the class of chemicals called xanthine. It has several physiological effects including stimulation of the central nervous system, heart, skeletal muscles, kidneys (causing increased urinary output), adrenal glands, and increased rate and depth of respiration. The peak blood level of caffeine occurs one to two hours after consumption, but increased alertness and perception with decreased fatigue occur almost immediately. The average adult gets a lift with 150-250 mg of caffeine.[7] Caffeine is a potent, addicting drug. Stopping caffeine suddenly may cause headaches and other withdrawal symptoms. Greater than 500 mg a day is considered heavy dosage.

CAFFEINE CONTENTS OF VARIOUS SUBSTANCES

	Mg/Oz.	8 Oz. Cup	12 Oz.
Drip Coffee	30	240 mg	
Percolated Coffee	22	176 mg	
Instant Coffee	16	128 mg	
Decaffeinated Coffee	1	8 mg	
Decaffeinated, Instant	1/2	4 mg	
Tea	2-10	16-80 mg	
Soft Drinks			
Mountain Dew			50 mg
Diet Pepsi			32 mg
Sunkist Orange			38 mg
Dr. Pepper			37 mg
Coca Cola			32 mg[8]
Hot Cocoa	13		
Vivarin (each tablet)	200		
Dexatrim	200		
NoDoz	100		
Excedrin	65		
Midol	30[9]		

Caffeine stimulates the release of norepinephrine and other brain neurotransmitters. This occurs in the brain and body and gives the lift associated with caffeine ingestion. With large long-term caffeine consumption, depletion of the neurotransmitters may result unless there is an ample supply of precursors or amino acids for replacement. Without replacement of these neurotrans-mitters, a caffeine user will begin to feel nervous and fatigued. Caffeine is believed to exert its biochemical effect by locking onto brain receptors producing a "relaxing" chemical called adenosine; this is responsible for the wake-up effect.

Caffeine interferes with the absorption and metabolism of Vitamin B1 or thiamine, thereby affecting our moods. Ingestion of large amounts of caffeine can eventually result in a Vitamin B1 deficiency.

One study showed that 300 mg of caffeine caused a 50 percent increase in the loss of magnesium and a 100 percent increase in the loss of calcium. Caffeine in the form of coffee and tea markedly inhibits iron absorption when taken with the meal or up to one hour following meals. A low iron level can contribute to depression.[10]

Caffeine Detox Procedure

1. Calculate daily caffeine consumption.
2. Keep a journal of how much caffeine is ingested from all sources. Physical dependency can occur on 5 or more cups per day.
3. Gradually taper off, perhaps using a procedure of gradual dilution. Here is a suggested schedule for withdrawal with a coffee mixture:
   Mix ¾ caffeine coffee and ¼ decaf for 3-7 days.
   Then ½ caffeine coffee and ½ decaf for 3-7 days.
   Then ¼ caffeine coffee and ¾ decaf for 3-7 days.
   Then decaf.

For soft drinks, simple reduce your intake on a

schedule such as the one above.

For pills/tablets, cut pills into halves or quarters.

Withdraw slowly from caffeine or you will experience unpleasant side effects such as headaches, shakes, stomach cramps, flushing, irritability, tension. Supplementing with GABA 750, the Stress and Anxiety Formula, and Esterified C may reduce any withdrawal symptoms.

V
Amino Acids
For Therapy

Amino acid supplements have a positive effect on people with addictive problems. Combinations of amino acids have been used to speed the healing of injuries and deficiencies to the body as a result of substance abuse. Amino acids also assist the body in handling the stress of recovery and can be continued to help prevent relapse of addiction.

The vast field of amino acid interactions is just beginning to unfold. For example, many of the amino acids are absorbed and metabolized in a similar fashion, and there is a great deal of competition between molecules; sometimes, one amino acid can cancel the effect of others, or they can inhibit one another's passage into the brain. This usually occurs among amino acids with similar structure. Taurine and glycine have the same function and compete for absorption.

Dietary amino acids will certainly affect the concentration of those neurotransmitters from which they are metabolically derived. So dopamine, norepinephrine, serotonin, histamine, and GABA can be increased or decreased depending upon excesses or deficiencies in their parent amino acids. Amino acid availability can affect the hypothalamus and its functions. A role for amino acids in behavior disorders has been identified; Methionine and its relationship with serotonin, tryptophan, glycine, and leucine is important for schizophrenia, sleep disorders, and affective disorders.

Among the indications with significance for brain function, choline is essential to the absorption of acetylcholine in the brain, and it can be regulated by dietary intake. Choline can affect important functions relating to learning and memory.

Functions of the nervous system depend upon the relationship between nutrients and brain function that will serve as a significant basis for behavioral pharmacological, and metabolic events.[1]

A recent theory published by Richard Bergland, M.D., a neurosurgeon, documents a decade of research which has yielded a modern view of the brain much as the ancient Greeks imagined it—as a hormonally modulated gland. The "stuff of thought," Dr. Bergland argues, is not electricity, as scientists of the last two thousand years have believed, but hormones; every time we move or laugh or cry, hormones spill into our brains, affecting our behavior. In that respect, the brain shares the same internal composition as the other organs of the body.

The realization that the brain is a gland, controlled by the hormones within it, is less than ten years old. It is suddenly clear that the unraveling of the mysteries of behavior can come through a better understanding of brain hormones. But more than that: many kinds of illnessnes, especially those related to stress, anxiety, and depression will be more easily treated by understanding the hormonal signals that move back and forth between the body and the brain. Many scientists believe that when a person goes into a state of extreme rage, the brain is filled with catecholamines, either adrenalin, noradrenalin, or serotonin. These could trigger the release of many other hormones, each of which could affect behavior and cloud a person's ability to make sound judgements. Fear, like rage, releases catecholamines and hormones, and the level of amino acids in the brain drops. Many addictive and behavioral diseases may result from a mistuned blood brain barrier that allows the brain to receive too few or too many amino acids.[2]

BRANCHED CHAIN AMINO ACIDS

Leucine, isoleucine, and valine are branched chain amino acids (BCAA). These three amino acids are critical to human life and are particularly involved in stress reactions, energy and muscle metabolism. BCAA are unique in that skeletal muscles use them directly as an energy source and they promote protein synthesis.

The branched chain amino acids, despite their structural similarities, have different metabolic routes. Valine goes solely to carbohydrates, leucine solely to fats, and isoleucine to both. A valine deficiency is noted by neurological defects in the brain, while an isoleucine deficiency is marked by muscle tremors. BCAA are useful because they are metabolized by the muscles. Stress states such as surgery, trauma, infections, fever, cirrhosis, and starvation require proportionally more leucine than with either valine or isoleucine. BCAA as well as other amino acids are commonly fed intravenously to malnourished patients. BCAA, especially leucine, stimulate protein synthesis, increase the reutilization of other amino acids in many organs, and decrease protein breakdown.

Stress can be analyzed into several levels, regardless of the stress source. As stress increases, total calories need to go up, primarily because protein—calorie needs increase. Thirty percent of the diet ideally should be protein or amino acids when the body is under severe stress; stress causes protein to break down faster. But when taken in supplement form, BCAA decreases the rate of breakdown of protein and amino acids.

A higher degree of stress requires more nutrients and, more specifically, BCAA and B6 or P5P (pyridoxine 5 phosphate). BCAA can replace the use of steroids which are commonly used by athletes, especially weight lifters. The levels of BCAA are lowered by such diseases as hepatitis, cirrhosis, hepatic coma, or liver disease; conversely, the aromatic amino acids tyrosine, tryptophan, and phenylalanine as well as methionine are increased in the same conditions.

BCAA, especially leucine, are great producers of energy under many kinds of stress—from trauma to surgery to infection, fever, muscle training, and weight lifting. Dosage will depend on your physical state and stress exhaustion. BCAA should be used in all stress situations. Normal dosage as a nutritional supplement would be 1 to 3 capsules daily or as directed by a health care professional. BCAA is available as a formula contained in one capsule.

GABA

Probably the least understood part of the entire limbic system is the ring of cerebral cortex called the limbic cortex. This part functions as a cross-over zone where signals are transmitted from the rest of the cortex into the limbic system. The function of the limbic cortex appears to be a link to the cerebral cortex for the control of behavior. Anxiety occurs when the limbic system—the part of the brain that stores anxiety messages—begins to release numerous signals, and, simultaneously, a physiological response starts to take place...the fight-or-flight syndrome. To an anxious person, this threatens a potential loss of control.

The unceasing alert signals from the limbic system eventually overwhelm the cortex. Then the ability of the cortex and the rest of the stress network to accommodate the crisis becomes exhausted. The balance between the limbic system and the cortex goes to pieces, often leading people into erratic or irrational fear...or making them want to reach for their favorite substance.

The ability of the cortex to communicate with the limbic system and the rest of the brain in an orderly fashion depends critically on inhibition, namely GABA (Gamma-Aminobutyric Acid) GABA inhibits the cells from firing, diminishing the excitatory messages reaching the frontal cortex. GABA seems to lower the excitatory level of the cell that is about to receive the incoming information. If the anxiety, stress, or fear continues, GABA's ability to block the message is decreased, and finally the process by which the signals are rated for priority breaks down and the frontal cortex is literally bombarded with anxiety messages. There follows a full-blown panic attack.

With the limbic system firing broadside fight-or-flight signals at the frontal cortex, the subject's ability to reason is diminished. The effects now can include fear of dying, pounding heart, sweating, trembling, tightness, weakness, loss of control, disorientation—the list is endless. Research has shown that GABA can actually mimic the tranquilizing effect of Valium and Librium but without the heavy sedation effect of these drugs. This information was first released for publication in 1982 in *Life Extension* by Sandy Shaw and Durk Pearson. Since that time, numerous studies have been published showing the successful use of GABA with anxiety-prone individuals and phobics. Many addicts, both drug and alcohol, have a tremendous problem with anxiety and anticipatory fear.

Research reports have shown that a person who constantly experiences "what-if" type anxiety, or what is termed "anticipatory fear," has empty GABA receptors in the brain. This means that the brain can be bombarded with random firings of excitatory messages. It is the receptor site in the brain that prevents the reception of all random firings so that the brain does not become overwhelmed. In *Lancet*, August 14, 1982, a research report about tranquilizers and GABA transmission clearly stated that GABA is a major inhibitory transmitter in the mammalian central nervous system and that the agents that raise the brain's GABA concentration possess a sedative anti-convulsant property.

After publication of information about GABA, the

public quickly became aware of the potentiality of GABA as an anti-anxiety formula. Survey of the medical journals shows over 300 articles (case studies, clinical reports, etc.) on GABA by orthomolecular psychiatrists and researchers.

GABA, and the neurons that utilize it as an inhibitory transmitter, is found throughout the central nervous system. In view of the growing knowledge regarding the regulation of the physiology of the central nervous system, GABA is assuming an ever-enlarging role as a major influence on drugs, in many cases replacing them (for example, Valium and Xanax). Preliminary pharmacological and clinical data have already demonstrated the usefulness of GABA in exploring human disease.[3]

As of 1986, clinical research at the Pain & Stress Center in San Antonio using pure GABA 750 mg, demonstrated the effectiveness of GABA as a muscle relaxant as well as an anti-anxiety agent. Pure GABA is tasteless, odorless, and colorless; it readily dissolves in water. In 100 clinical trials done at the Pain & Stress Center with patients, GABA 750 reduced the level of tension in the muscles in 7 minutes. Additionally, GABA is helpful in reducing anxiety and can help to break up an anxiety attack.

Dr. K.J. Berman at Mt. Sinai School of Medicine published an extensive review in *Clinical Neuropharmacology* (1985) entitled "Progabide: A New GABA Mimetric Electric Agent in Clinical Use." Dr. Berman sums up the research and results of the chemistry, the role of GABA, and the influences in the central nervous system. In 1985 the most valid research published on GABA relates to anxiety. In 1988 GABA's benefits are still being explored. GABA not only aids anxiety sufferers, but also lessens muscle tension, and aids Parkinson's symptoms, as well as inhibiting the desire for alcohol and cocaine.[4] Soon this extremely versatile amino acid will make more major contributions to aid those suffering from pain, stress, anxiety, and addiction.

L-GLUTAMINE,
THE SURPRISING BRAIN FUEL

Tests have shown that glutamic acid, a "non-essential" amino acid, improves intelligence, speeds the healing of ulcers, gives a "lift" from fatigue, and helps control alcoholism, schizophrenia, and the craving for sweets. The problem is that in order to get more of this amino acid into the brain where it becomes a high-energy brain fuel, we have to use a little nutritional ingenuity. If more glutamic acid is transported into the brain it might make a person smarter.

The brain has a protective barrier that lets in only a very few chemicals. Glutamic acid, like all amino acids with but one exception, is poorly carried across this protective blood barrier. Even when more glutamic acid is eaten, little more ends up in the brain. Fortunately, the body can make other compounds out of the amino acids, and some of these new compounds <u>can</u> cross the barrier. Thus the brain can make some glutamic acid out of other chemical building blocks that are transported into the brain, and some glutamic acid can cross the barrier.

When the proper building blocks are not in the diet in sufficient quantities, or the individual is not efficient in making glutamic acid in the brain, or has problems in carrying glutamic acid across the barrier, that person is never as efficient as he or she could be. Other more serious problems may be caused.

Dr. Roger Williams in *Nutrition Against Disease* tells of the limited success of one researcher who administered glutamic acid to retarded children and schizophrenics, and wonders what greater improvement would have been obtained if the investigator had only known that another amino acid—the amide, glutamine—can readily cross the blood-barrier into the brain where it is quickly converted into glutamic acid.

Although taking large amounts of glutamic acid produces only a trivial elevation of this acid in the brain, taking moderate amount of 1-glutamine produces a marked elevation.

Glutamic Acid Function

Glutamic acid has a unique function in brain metabolism that makes it of major importance. Glutamic acid is not made into brain chemicals called neurotransmitters, as are some amino acids, nor is it incorporated into protein structures in the brain. Glutamic acid has two major functions. The unique surprise is that glutamic acid serves primarily as a fuel for the brain, a feat which only one other compound, glucose (blood sugar), can perform.

The second major function of glutamic acid is that throughout the body glutamic acid, with its ability to pick up excess ammonia and be converted into glutamine, serves as a buffer against excess ammonia and in regulating the compounds that enter into a series of vital reactions called the "citric acid cycle."

The relationship of glutamic acid to glucose goes beyond their brain-fuel interrelationship. Glutamic acid restores hypoglycemic patients in insulin coma to consciousness at a lower blood sugar level than when glucose alone is used.[5]

The brain can store only a small reserve of glucose. Therefore, the brain is very dependent on the second-to-second supply of blood sugar. This explains the dizziness and other nervous symptoms in hypoglycemics.

Glutamic acid is the only other compound that the brain uses for energy. The gray matter in the brain contains a special enzyme to convert glutamic acid to a compound that regulates brain cell activity. Glutamic acid is used in a special high-energy reaction that by-passes the normal energy-producing chemistry of the citric acid cycle.

Thus, a shortage of L-glutamine in the diet or glutamic acid in the brain results in brain damage due to "excess ammonia" or a brain that can never get into "high-gear."

Alcoholism

Dr. Roger Williams has been the pioneer in L-glutamine research, but he is quick to point out that his colleagues at the Clayton Foundation for Research at the University of Texas made the initial discovery that aroused his interest.

Dr. William Shive discovered that L-glutamine protected bacteria cells against poisoning by alcohol.[6] Then Dr. Williams, together with his associates Drs. L.L. Rogers and R.B. Pelton, made the all-important observation that not only did L-glutamine protect individuals against the poisonous effects of alcohol, it also stopped their **craving** for alcohol. [7] [8]

This property of L-glutamine has been studied carefully and its effect cannot be questioned.[9] It has been compared with its chemical relatives glutamic acid, asparagic, and the simpler amino acid, glycine. These other substances had no effect whatever, but L-glutamine consistently decreased alcohol consumption.

One alcoholic stopped drinking when 3000 mg of L-glutamine was administered daily without the patient's knowledge.[10] (L-glutamine is tasteless and can be mixed with food or water without detection.) Dr. Lorene Rogers reported several cases in which L-glutamine was successful, and placebos ineffective.[11]

Recently, glutamine was discovered to help stop the craving for sweets. This is not surprising since the same appetite control center in the brain (the hypothalamus) that is protected against upset by sugar, is protected against upset by alcohol.

Dr. Shive found that L-glutamine shortened the healing time for ulcers.[12] Dr. H.L. Newbold recommends L-glutamine to fight fatigue, depression, and impotence.[13] L-glutamine is also of benefit to patients with petit mal epilepsy.[14] Dr. Abram Hoffer has used L-glutamine with other nutrients successfully against schizophrenia, senility, and mental retardation.[15]

Dosage

Dr. Williams recommends one to four grams (1000 to 4000 mg) a day. It is safe to say that more could be better, and that no one is likely to take enough to do the slightest damage since L-glutamine is a natural and harmless food substance.[16] [17]

Dr. H.L. Newbold advises, "If you want to take it just for a potential lift, begin at one 200 mg capsule three times a day, for a week, increasing to two capsules three times a day the second week as part of your experimental nutrition regimen.

"If you are trying to control a drinking problem, take (1000 mg) three times a day with 50 mg of B6 daily."[18]

Availability

L-glutamine is available as a food supplement in 500 mg capsules to meet the increasing needs of physicians for their schizophrenic and alcoholic patients. The proven clinical success of L-glutamine warrants a new look by researchers hoping to improve brain function.

PHENYLALANINE

Currently, ten to fifteen compounds have been identified as neurotransmitters. As far as we know, not all of these transmitters are affected by diet, but there are three that are definitely related to dietary control. These are norepinephrine, acetylcholine and serotonin.

Another amino acid, phenylalanine, is one of the essential amino acids, and it is necessary for life. It is a precursor to norepinephrine; norepinephrine functions both as a stimulatory neurotransmitter and as a brain hormone. The formation of these transmitters is affected by diet, by making more or less of the respective precursors which are available to the brain.[19] The rate that each of these is synthesized is affected by the availability of the particular substance. As a result, the rate of synthesis of serotonin that is immediately available to the brain is predisposed by the amount of amino acid presursors, phenylalanine, and tyrosine.[20]

L-phenylalanine is the raw substance that produces several compounds of the catecholamine family of compounds which are responsible for the transmission of nerve impulses; provided that a good supply of phenylalanine (or tyrosine) is in the blood, the adrenal medulla and the nerve cells can rapidly produce these catecholamines. L-phenylalanine is one of the essential nutrients for life. All of the amino acids are the building blocks of protein, but phenylalanine is one of the few amino acids that is readily converted into the brain compounds that control a person's moods.

CONVERSION PATH OF PHENYLALANINE

L-phenylalanine---- ► L-tyrosine---- ► Dopa---- ► Dopamine

Norepinephrine

Epinephrine

Phenylalanine is required in the body to rebuild proteins; its most important role may be in the production of the critical hormones epinephrine (adrenalin), dopa, norepinephrine, dopamine, thyroxine, and tri-iodothyronine. Phenylalanine is found in a variety of foods in small amounts. Inadequate amounts of phenylalanine lead to low levels of norepinephrine which can result in severe depression. Since phenylalanine is converted to tyrosine, dopa, dopamine, norepinephrine, and epinephrine, these compounds are called, as a whole, neurotransmitters. They control the whole basic process of nerve impulse transmission. Epinephrine is important because it is excreted at the nerve terminals in the hypothalamus and norepinephrine is excreted at the sympathetic nerve endings giving a basic fight-or-flight response. Thus it affects the immediate post-synaptic cells.[21]

Norepinephrine is the principal neurotransmitter at the peripheral nerve endings of the sympathetic nervous system; norepinephrine is the neurotransmitter in certain central synapses and is stored in the presynaptic vesicles. When the nerve receives an appropraite impulse, the storage vesicle which is bound to the cell membrane releases its contents (norepinephrine) to bridge the gap between the pre- and post-synaptic neurons. Calcium is necessary for the binding of the released neurotransmitter. The norepinephrine then reversely attaches itself to the receptors on the external surface of the post-synaptic membrane. This transmitter-receptor complex activates adenylate cyclase located on the internal surface of the membrane. The conversion of adenosine tri-phosphate (ATP) to cyclic AMP is accomplished by adenylate cyclase.

Norepinephrine is activated in part by the enzymatic breakdown. The extraneural enzyme (catechol-o-methyl-transferase or COMT) part is inactivated by the intraneuronal (mitochondrial) enzyme (monoamine oxidase or MAO) in the pre-synaptic nerve terminal. But the greatest portion is captured and replaced into the pre-synaptic cell and the storage vesicles. Part is activated by the intraneuronal enzyme MAO) in the pre-synaptic nerve terminal.[22]

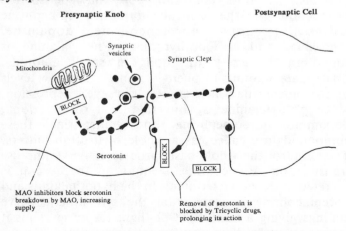

Presynaptic Knob

Postsynaptic Cell

Synaptic vesicles

Synaptic Clept

Mitochondria

BLOCK

Serotonin

BLOCK

BLOCK

MAO inhibitors block serotonin breakdown by MAO, increasing supply

Removal of serotonin is blocked by Tricyclic drugs, prolonging its action

Neuropharmacology of Serotonin Synapses of Inhibitory Pathway

Whenever the body is under a tremendous amount of stress, an enormous load is placed on the adrenal glands; many times, the epinephrine and norepinephrine levels—especially the norepinephrine levels—are either very low or depleted. Low levels of norepinephrine can cause depression, and stress can cause pain, depression, anxiety, uncertainty, and fear.

A person who is depressed may become more depressed when he is alone or in a particular situation which gives rise to distraction. He has no happiness in his life, and there is a feeling of hopelessness and helplessness as to what the future holds. He has no energy. He has no interests. Often he will reach for a drink or drug.

Most alcoholics are depressed. Changes of appetite are quite normal, either to one extreme or the other—i.e., undereating or overeating.[23] Depression exhibits many faces. It constitutes a wide spectrum from sadness or the "blues" that everyone experiences at one time or another through reactive depression caused by the loss of someone or something loved. It extends to psychotic depression in which contact with reality is lost, and there may even be thoughts of suicide or—the ultimate loss—the actual act of suicide. Psychotic depression may or may not be endogenous (i.e., self-produced) depression.[24] It can actually be diet induced. Depression is one of the most common disorders of the mind. Often it is treated with anti-depressants and/or tranquilizers.

The affective disorders are divided into two types: unipolar and bipolar. Unipolar is characterized by depression or mania alone. Bipolar is depicted by both depression and mania. The difference is important, for the origin is probably different; likewise, the two disorders have different pharmacological responses.

The widely accepted hypothesis for affective disorders is the catecholamine hypothesis. Although it has various forms, the simplest is that the depression is caused by a metabolism. More evidence is available for the depression than the mania to support the theory. In traditional medicine, the depression is treated with monoamine oxidase inhibitors (MAO's); the inhibitors are believed to exercise their effects by inhibiting the breakdown of norepinephrine.

Another drug used to treat depression is the tricyclic anti-depressant which prevents the re-uptake of the norepinephrine, dopamine, and serotonin from the synaptic cleft. Still another medication used in this treatment is the psychostimulants such as amphetamine and methylphenidate. These drugs work by increasing the amount of norepinephrine available at the synaptic cleft. The increased norepinephrine is via increased release from the storage vesicles, inhibiting monoamine re-uptake. To date, a single mechanism does not fit all the facts of the affective disorders and their pharmacological and therapeutic responses. The cause of depression does not appear to be a single entity.[25]

L-phenylalanine had been used to increase the level of norepinephrine in the brain. The neurotransmitters, especially norepinephrine, are responsible for an elevation and positive moods, alertness and ambition in a person. Sometimes the norepinephrine level is artificially elevated by drugs such as anti-depressants; these drugs work by blocking the norepinephrines from re-entering the pouches within the neuron. This blocking causes the artificial manipulation which leads to an elevation of the mood. In actuality, this aggravates the original problem. The natural way to normalize the brain and nerve level of norepinephrine is by providing adequate levels in the diet in the form of L-phenylalanine or L-tyrosine or with supplementation of these amino acids.[26]

DLPA AND DEPRESSION

Most people think of their emotions as separate from their bodies and unconnected with the chemistry of their brain cells. However, depression, irritability, and anxiety are all reflections of the functioning of the of the brain. When certain nutrients are not supplied to the brain, it experiences an array of negative emotions, tending to lose its coping ability in response to the stressful circumstances we confront each day of our lives.

Although the brain is only equal to two percent of our total body weight, 25% of our total metabolic activity takes place there. This is probably the reason that the brain is so sensitive to nutritional deficiency. In fact, our need for proper brain function is so great that the body feeds the brain preferentially.

Nutrients can cause important changes in the chemical composition of substances in the brain, with corresponding changes in our feelings. Scientific studies show that by taking particular amino acids, mental depression, apathy, peevishness, and the desire to be left alone can be alleviated.

About one in five Americans has significant symptoms of depression, more than 1.5 million are being treated for it, and about 30 million can expect to suffer from it at some point in their lives. Classic, full-blown depression has been described as "the loss of the capacity to enjoy life combined with a poverty of thought and movement." It can appear as grief, but may manifest itself through a series of emotional states so extreme that the outcome is suicide or total withdrawal.

Of course a preoccupation with death or suicide is an obvious symptom, but often depression is not obvious because the person does not feel "sad." This is called "masked depression." Symptoms may involve changes in sleeping patterns, such as insomnia, early morning waking, constant sleepiness, or changes in eating patterns—either overeating or loss of appetite. The person may be anxious or have excessive complaints about body functions and chronic pain, especially headaches, but also indigestion or constipation. Both hair and skin may feel dry and lose luster, while blood pressure has a tendency to be high. There is an inability to enjoy customary pleasures and a concomitant loss of sex drive, loss of energy, extreme fatigue, difficulty concentrating and making decisions, irritability, and possibly temperamental outbursts.

With endogenous depression, there are symptoms of guilt, self-hate, feelings of worthlessness, apathy, crying spells, and a desire to be left alone. Women are more susceptible to depression than men—1 woman in 6, compared to 1 man in 12. It is thought that there may be some connection to the female reproductive cycles. There are also some diseases, such as hypothyroidism (underactive thyroid gland), that may produce depression, while others, such as arthritis or heart disease, commonly bring on a depressive reaction. Overall, not only can depression be a result of nutritional deficiency, but that depression in turn puts a further stress on the body. Without the proper nutritional attention, depression has a very deleterious effect on the general health.

Treatment

DLPA (or DL-phenylalanine) has been found to be effective in the treatment of depression. Studies since 1974 show it to be particularly beneficial in cases of endogenous depression. This is the type of depression that is characterized by a decrease in energy and interest, feelings of worthlessness, and a pervasive sense of helplessness to control the course of one's life. Significant improvement has also been achieved with people suffering from reactive depression (thought to be caused by environmental influences such as a death in the family) and involutional depression (an aging-related depression). DLPA has also shown itself to be effective for other types of depression, including the depressive phase of manic-depression, schizophrenic depression, and post-amphetamine depression.

Phenylalanine is one of the "essential" amino acids, and it must be obtained through the diet. The type of phenylalanine our bodies require is L-phenylalanine, while the type found to be most effective against depression is D-phenylalanine. D-phenylalanine mirrors L-phenylalanine in its molecular structure. DLPA or the DL-form is the preferable form for depression. DLPA is a 50/50 mixture of D-phenylalanine and L-phenylalanine. They do not interact but follow separate transport and metabolic pathways. In other words, 500 mg of DLPA behaves like 250 mg of pure D-phenylalanine plus 250 mg of L-phenylalanine.

At this time, it appears that DLPA has three separate anti-depressant effects in the body: increased production of PEA, increased endorphin levels, and increased norepinephrine production. These biochemical changes are not isolated but rather create a synergistic overlap which accounts for the terrific result of DLPA in the treatment of depression.

Although D-phenylalanine is very rare in nature, all mammals, including man, are able to metabolize it. Part of the metabolic process involves conversion to phenylethylamine or PEA. It seems to be a natural stimulant. This characteristic prompted mental health researchers to speculate that a deficiency of PEA in the nervous system might be a cause of depression. This concept gained support when research demonstrated that depressed patients were not just low in PEA, they were "immeasurably low."

In a series of studies in the late 70's, it was also found that every major treatment for depression indirectly elevated levels of PEA in the brain. Both D-and L- forms of phenylalanine are directly converted to PEA. However, D-phenylalanine has been reported to induce greater, more prolonged increases than L-phenylalanine alone.

A second way in which DLPA may act as an anti-depressant is in its ability to inhibit enzymes which break down the endorphin hormone. Endorphins are morphine-like hormones whose presence may account for the euphoria experienced by runners, joggers, and other enthusiasts of aerobic expercise.[27] It is thought that endorphin concentration in the brain may be critical in mood regulation. If a sufficient number of the receptors in the brain are filled with endorphins and enkephalins, a person feels a sense of well-being. But, if for some reason the endorphin level is reduced and too few receptors are filled, the deficiency causes a person to feel a sense of urgency and irritation. In a similar way if the production is too high and an excessive number of receptors are filled, a person feels a sense of euphoria that is usually followed by a letdown. This is natural, and is a major cause of the "ups and down" everyone experiences in life.

If a drug such as heroin or morphine is consumed, these drugs take the place of endorphins and enkephalins at the receptors and, if taken in quantity, activate a large number of receptors, creating an unnatural euphoria. A person feels great for a while, but the drug has a serious side effect. It causes the body to shut down the production of natural endorphins and enkephalins. Then, as the drug wears off, the feeling of need becomes greater than ever. If drug consumption continues over a period of time, the ability of the body to produce endorphins and enkephalins is reduced, and the person becomes dependent on the drug.[28]

A patient who has been taking narcotics or drugs for a while has desensitized his endorphin receptors. Even if he desired to quit using the narcotics, his body would not respond to an endorphin release. He must gradually reduce his intake of drugs to slowly reactivate his endorphin receptor sites.

In fact, clinical research has shown that endorphins administered intravenously can trigger sudden, dramatic anti-depressant actions, even in suicidal patients. Essentially, DLPA works because it inhibits endorphin-degrading enzymes so that the endorphins produced by the brain last longer.

You will recall that alcohol has been found to cause the production of chemicals called tetrahydroisoquino-lines, or TIQ's, which have effects similar to morphine or heroin. They fill the enkephalin receptors, produce an unnatural euphoria, and reduce the output of the natural endorphins and enkephalins. The long-term use of large amounts of alcohol produces a permanent, urgent need for alcohol, and the craving for more alcohol or another drink.

Additionally, DLPA could be converted to the brain neurotransmitter norepinephrine. A deficiency of norepinephrine was the first brain chemical deficiency believed to be involved in severe depression. Like PEA, norepinephrine is a natural stimulant. Both D- and L-phenylalanine serve as its precursors, although they follow somewhat different metabolic pathways. Most anti-depressant drugs are designed to increase the amount of norepinephrine in the central nervous system, but by very different means than DLPA.

Anti-depressant drugs, such as tricyclics, can be effective in reducing symptoms of depression. Unfortunately, this is where their usefulness ends. They can engender numerous adverse side effects such as seizures, drowsiness, nausea, and anorexia. They can also stimulate neurotransmitter release for mood elevation, but they prevent reabsorption of the neuro-transmitters into nerve terminals. This depletes our cellular stores of neurotransmitter material and inter-feres with proper brain function. DLPA can serve to restore brain levels to normal.

In a recent double-blind controlled study, DLPA was found to be equally as effective as the tricyclic drug imipramine, the most commonly prescribed anti-depressant. Psychopathological, neurologic, and somatic indices showed no differences between the two treatments. Side effects tended to be higher for the imipramine patients.

- DL-phenylalanine and imipramine were given to depressed patients in equal dosages (150-200 mg.day) with 20 patients in each group.

- Psychopathological, neurologic, and somatic indices showed no differences between the two treatments.

- Automatic side effects "tended to be higher for the

imipramine patients."

- Anti-depressant efficacy of DL-phenylalanine "seems to equal that of the tricyclic anti-depressant imipramine."

Evidence indicates that DLPA may be useful in alleviating the mood disorders associated with PMS (premenstrual syndrome). Reports from clinical investigations have revealed that over 80% of all patients suffering from PMS have experienced good to complete relief.

DLPA dosage comes in capsules of 375 to 750 mg. The dosage is generally 4 to 8 capsules prior to meals. It is important that the capsules be taken in divided dosages throughout the day to get the anti-depressant effect. Dosage can be varied with improvement, but must be individualized. People who suffer from PKU (phenyketonuria) should not use DLPA.

KEY FACTORS OF DLPA

1) DLPA is a highly safe, nontoxic substance when used in short- or long-term therapy.

2) DLPA does not induce excessive excitation or arousal in normal or depressed subjects.

3) Toxic overdose is impossible and there is generally a lack of potential for abuse.

4) DLPA does not cause adverse side effects.

Endogenous depression, which was discussed earlier in relation to DLPA, is a particularly insidious mental state. The person involved feels so worthless that they do not want to take the necessary steps to feel good. When a person feels depressed, they do not feel like taking good care of themselves. Of course, that is the very time a person needs to do right—eat right, sleep right, think right, and...get enough exercise and amino acids.[29]

L-TYROSINE

Recent clinical findings that the natural amino acid L-tyrosine is helpful in overcoming depression, improving memory, and increasing mental alertness, has stimulated interest in the nutritional role of this dietary factor. Of particular interest is the research linking L-tyrosine deficiency to the development of depression in some oral contraceptive users.

The body needs L-tyrosine to build many complex structural proteins and enzymes. But recent clinical research has centered on the simpler compounds used by the body to transmit nerve impulses which determine a person's mental mood and alertness. These compounds are called neurotransmitters, and they are readily formed in the body by minor alteration of the L-tyrosine molecule. It is very likely that deficiencies of L-tyrosine can impair the body's ability to produce the proper balance of these neurotransmitters.[30]

In assessing the dietary quantity of L-tyrosine, the L-phenylalanine content of the diet should also be determined, as the body can make L-tyrosine out of "leftover" L-phenylalanine. Dietary L-tyrosine can spare the body some (but not all) of its L-phenylalanine need. The best food sources of L-tyrosine are meats, eggs, and dairy products. Clinical researchers prefer to use L-tyrosine supplements rather than rely on whole foods because it is difficult to obtain such amounts in normal diets.

L-tyrosine (or its presursor, L-phenylalanine) is used by the body to produce several compounds which are important to nerve transmission. The adrenal medulla and nerve cells can quickly produce these compounds from L-tyrosine. The conversions proceed as follows:[31]

L-tyrosine-- ►dopa-- ►dopamine-- ►norepinephrine-- ►epinephrine

Two of these compounds, epinephrine and norepinephrine, have wide ranging activities that affect brain and nerve cells. Both compounds are produced in nerve cells, as well as in the adrenal medulla where they can be stored. A third compound produced from L-tyrosine, dopamine, affects nerve tracts in the brain, in addition to its role in the production of the other two.[32]

These compounds are called neurotransmitters because they control the basic process of impulse transmission between nerve cells. Epinephrine is secreted at nerve terminals in the hypothalamus. Norepinephrine is released at sympathatic nerve (fight-or-flight response) endings, and thus affects the immediate postsynaptic cells. Dopamine transmission appears to be defective in Parkinson's disease.

These neurotransmitters are responsible for an elevated and positive mood, alertness, and ambition. Medical researchers in the past have relied on increasing the brain and nerve levels of norepinephrine by using drugs, such as phenylpropanolamine and amphetamines, which cause the release of norepinephrine, block its return to storage, or slow the destruction of L-tyrosine. However, such artificial manipulation often leads to depletion of the neurotransmitter and the aggravation of the original problem. The natural solution is to normalize brain and nerve levels of norepinephrine by providing adequate levels of dietary L-tyrosine.[33]

Clinical studies have shown that L-tyrosine controls medication-resistant depression. Two studies published in 1980 are of interest. The first was published in the *American Journal of Psychiatry* by Dr. Alan J. Gelenberg of the Department of Psychiatry at Harvard Medical School. Dr. Gelenberg discussed the role of L-tyrosine in controlling anxiety and depression. He postulated that a lack of available L-tyrosine results in a deficiency of the hormone norepinephrine at a specific brain location, which, in turn, relates to mood problems such as depression.

Dr. Gelenberg treated patients having long-standing depression not responding to standard therapy by administering dietary supplements of L-tyrosine. Within two weeks of daily intakes of 100 milligrams per day of an L-tyrosine supplement tremendous improvement was noted. Patients were able to discontinue or reduce amphetamines to minimal levels in a matter of weeks.

The second study was published in *Lancet* by Dr. I. Goldberg. Allergy sufferers have also responded well to L-tyrosine supplementation, as well as those on weight loss programs. Pearson reports that L-tyrosine supplementation is a preferred way to control appetite, rather than phenylpropanolamine or amphetamine administration which causes norepinephrine release only.[34]

Cocaine addiction has been helped with daily supplementation of doses of at least 3000 mg per day in divided dosages. Additionally, GABA in doses of 3000 mg per day has reduced the stress and anxiety associated with cocaine addiction. Other important amino acids and nutrients include DLPA—2000 mg per day, Siberian ginseng—1000-1500 mg per day, glutamine—2000 mg per day.

L-TRYPTOPHAN

Tryptophan is an essential amino acid which is the precursor of serotonin. Serotonin is synthesized from tryptophan. Serotonin is a brain neurotransmitter, platelet clotting factor, and neurohormone found in the organs throughout the body. Tryptophan is essential to maintain the body's protein balance. When food that is protein deficient or lacking tryptophan is fed to growing or mature individuals, such foods fail to replace worn-out materials which are lost by the body during the organic activities of its cells, tissues, and organs. The amino acid tryptophan is used up in the vital activities of the body, and in turn, must be replaced to prevent atrophy of the body's structures.

Tryptophan is one of the few substances capable of passing the blood-brain barrier.[35] It has a variety of important roles in mental activity. When tryptophan intake is deficient, especially during periods of stress, serotonin levels drop, yielding depression, anxiety, insecurity, hyperactivity, insomnia, and pain. To have enough tryptophan, the body must have an ample supply of Vitamin B6, without which tryptophan cannot be formed.[36]

Tryptophan's role in behavior has been demonstrated by the number of mental functions that it directly influences. Serotonin produces a relaxed, calm, secure, mellow, and morphine-like analgesic feeling. Hyperactive children/adults have a low serotonin level. Supplements containing tryptophan and Vitamin B6 can correct some of the biochemical disorders related to aggression.

Studies have been done at the Pain & Stress Therapy Center in San Antonio with people who demonstrated a wide range of hyperactive behavior from the inability to concentrate, anxiety, insecurity, aggression, insomnia, fear, and withdrawal. When the patients were supplemented with tryptophan, GABA, B6, and other vitamins, behavior changes were noted within 72 hours, all in a positive direction. When their brain chemistry was adjusted to meet deficiencies, their behavior changed to calm and relaxed.

Another significant finding in studies done with tryptophan demonstrated that low levels of serotonin could play a part in the development of depression.[37] When tryptophan (2000 mg) at bedtime is combined with tyrosine in doses of 3,000 mg per day, they can mimic the effects of most antidepressants. Tryptophan is useful in unipolar depression or constant, low-grade depression with no highs or lows.[38]

Both depression and pain can have a profound effect on the ability of a person to fall asleep. Difficulty in falling asleep can be caused by low serotonin levels. But tryptophan has been shown to be very effective in insomnia problems, reducing the time needed to fall asleep and increasing the number of hours spent sleeping. The usual dosage is 500 to 2000 mg taken one hour prior to bedtime with a carbohydrate such as orange juice or fruit.[39]

*****

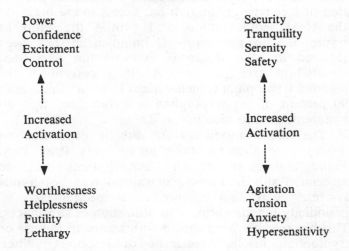

EXCITATORY SYSTEM	INHIBITORY SYSTEM
PLEASURE	
Power	Security
Confidence	Tranquility
Excitement	Serenity
Control	Safety
↑	↑
Increased Activation	Increased Activation
↓	↓
Worthlessness	Agitation
Helplessness	Tension
Futility	Anxiety
Lethargy	Hypersensitivity

PAIN

<u>**PAIN AND PLEASURE MODEL**[40]</u>
*****

Because serotonin is a neurotransmitter, it is one of the most important chemicals that helps control moods as well. Best of all, tryptophan is safe and is a natural relaxant and tranquilizer of the central nervous system. The body has no difficulty in rapidly metabolizing and clearing it from the body. It is an essential amino acid which is necessary for life, and is the sole precursor for serotonin. It does not simply pass through the gut into the brain to become serotonin. It must compete with five other amino acids—tyrosine, phenylalanine, leucine, isoleucine, and valine—at the blood brain barrier. In order to increase the amount of brain serotonin, the ratio of tryptophan must be elevated out of proportion to the competing amino acids. Metabolism and protein intake may alter this ratio.

About 90 percent of serum tryptophan is bound to albumin. Free fatty acids (serum) share the same albumin binding sites. Changing both the blood sugar level and insulin may increase and decrease the proportion of free tryptophan that has access to the brain. In the total serum amino acid profile the ratio of tryptophan to the nutrient amino acids has been elevated in each instance. Tyrosine has also been elevated in each instance. About 1 percent of the ingested tryptophan is metabolized to serotonin. About 90 percent of the tryptophan is metabolized through kynurenic acid to nicotinic acid.[41]

The neurotransmitters are directly dependent on dietary tryptophan and other amino acids. It has been found that there are circadian rhythms that are associated with the amino acid utilization in the nervous system.[42] Circadian rhythm is a specific type of periodicity for the uptake and utilization of substances. This has recently been shown with regard to the use of tryptophan in the treatment of insomnia. When tryptophan is used during the day it does not seem to induce sleep, only a calm relaxed state; but when taken near bedtime it seems to induce sleep, as shown in sleep studies done at several medical centers. This seems to indicate that tryptophan's uptake across the blood-brain barrier is tied to the circadian rhythms of the sleep cycle, and its absorption is facilitated in the brain in its conversion to serotonin more effectively during times when a person would normally sleep. This is why it is clinically suggested to administer tryptophan at bedtime if it is to be used for treating sleep disorders. Conversely, tryptophan or tyrosine should be used during the day to treat certain forms of depression.

Two researchers in England compared the antidepressant effects of tryptophan and Tofranil (Tofranil is a drug which is commonly used for depression.) Both groups of patients with depression improved. The conclusions of their study revealed trypophan was just as effective as the laboratory-produced drug, and there were no side effects from the tryptophan. Conversely, the side effects for the Tofranil group included blurring of the vision, dryness of the mouth, low blood pressure, urinary retention, heart palpitations, hepatitis, and seizures.[43]

L-tryptophan is obtained in the diet everyday. Many rich natural forms of tryptophan include: bananas, green leafy vegetables, red meat, milk, pineapple, avocados, and eggs. Large doses of tryptophan when combined with niacinamide and vitamin B6 can enhance the conversion of tryptophan to serotonin.[44]

Amino acids have an impact on brain neuro-chemistry; they actually influence neuro-regulatory substances that may ultimately clinically cause changes in mind, mood, memory, and behavior.[45]

L-CYSTINE

Research is focusing on the protective role of dietary amino acids. L-cystine is of interest, not only because it builds proteins such as those in hair, but because it helps destroy harmful chemicals in the body such as acetaldehyde and free radicals produced by smoking and drinking. The natural form of cystine found in foods is designated L-cystine.[46]

L-cystine is the stable form of the sulfur-containing amino acid cysteine. Both forms are amino acids, and the body readily interconverts one into the other as needed. Thus, the two forms may be considered as a single amino acid in metabolism.

Cysteine is more soluble in water than L-cystine, but both are very soluble in acid solutions.[47] However, solubility should not be confused with digestibility or assimilation.

L-cystine spares methionine (another important amino acid) and can completely replace dietary methionine if the diet is supplemented by appropriate amounts of folic acid and vitamin B12.

L-cystine is abundant in proteins such as keratin in hair (12%) and trypsinogen (10%). Moderate amounts are found in the enzyme papain (4%) and the milk protein lactoglobulin (3%). Lesser amounts of L-cystine are in hemoglobin (1%), albumin (1%), carboxypeptidase (1%), and edestin (1%).[48] Many important biological compounds (e.g., glutathione, coenzyme A) depend on the sulfur provided by L-cystine. The important selenium containing the enzyme glutathione peroxidase is largely cystèine. L-cystine has been used as a food supplement and as a detoxicant. Heavy metals such as mercury, lead and cadmium will be "tied up" by either the sulfur released by L-cystine or by the sulfhydryl group in L-cystine.

Heavy drinkers and smokers may be protected by L-cystine against acetaldehyde poisoning from chronic alcohol intake or smoking, according to Dr. Herbert Sprince and his associates at the Veterans Administration Hospital, Coatesville, Pennsylvania, and Thomas Jefferson Univesity, Philadelphia, Pennsylvania. At the 1974 meeting of the Federation óf American Societies for Experimental Biology, they reported that cysteine (L-cystine) and vitamin C gave 100 percent protection against a standard lethal dose of acetaldehyde in rats.

Pearson reports that this amino acid is effective "not only in preventing hangovers, but also in preventing brain and liver damage from alcohol, and in preventing damage such as emphysema and cancer caused by smoking."[49]

L-cystine has been found to offer a degree of protection against radiation.[50]

Recently, Dr. William Philpott has postulated that L-cystine is necessary for the utilization of vitamin B-6. His studies suggest that "a majority of chronic degenerative illnesses, whether physical or mental, have a vitamin B-6 utilization disorder. The culprit in this B-6 utilization problem seems to be L-cystine deficiency."[51] Dr. Philpott recommends patients having the vitamin

B-6 utilization problem take 1.5 grams of L-cystine three times a day for a month and then reduce it to twice a day.

L-CARNITINE

Recent research indicates that L-carnitine plays an important role in converting stored body fat into energy, controlling hypoglycemia, energizing the heart, reducing angina attacks, and is beneficial to patients having diabetes, liver disease, or kidney disease.

L-carnitine hardly received any attention at all from nutritionists until 1973, nearly seven decades after its discovery. Early research indicated that L-carnitine was essential to the diet, and it was classified as a vitamin and designated Vitamin B-t. Later, it was discovered that the body produced L-carnitine from two essential amino acids, L-lysine and L-methionine, provided that sufficient amounts of Vitamins B3 and B6, and C, plus the mineral iron, are present. Since L-carnitine can be produced in the well-nourished person, nutritionists assumed that everyone either produced all of the L-carnitine that they needed or they received sufficient dietary carnitine to augment that produced in the body to meet its needs. In 1973, it was determined that an L-carnitine deficiency can exist in people for various reasons. Now the thinking has almost come a full circle with the recent evidence strongly suggesting that L-carnitine may be essential to the newborn.

As the role of L-carnitine in health became clearer, researchers became more interested. During the 1970's there were approximately 600 studies published concerning biochemistry of L-carnitine, but none of these studies actually addressed the role of L-carnitine as a nutrient. However, between 1980 and 1983, nearly 300 studies have been published including a significantly large number investigating L-carnitine nutritive and anomalies of L-carnitine metabolism that result in clinical symptoms.

L-carnitine is an amino acid in which "methyl" groups replace the hydrogen atoms of the "amino" group.

The enzymes that use L-carnitine as a substrate are critical to energy production. L-carnitine's primary role is to transport large fat molecules into the portion of the cell where the fats can be converted into energy. In the absence of L-carnitine, many fats cannot be "burned" and they build up within the cell and the bloodstream as triglycerides and fats.[52] L-carnitine-deficient people often have severe bouts of hypoglycemia. The sugar addict and the alcoholic have been known to have problems with hypoglycemia. When the blood sugar drops, the person may reach for a drink to rapidly increase his blood sugar; hypoglycemia is one of the multitude of theories about the causes of alcoholism and addiction.[53]

L-carnitine plays an important role in the production of heat in "brown fat." "Brown fat" is the fat tissue that helps us acclimate to cold temperatures, and is thought to help determine how much of the food we eat is burned for heat and how much is converted into stored body-fat. L-carnitine also prevents ketones from accumulating to cause "acid blood" during poor weight-loss diets. This condition is called ketosis, and when uncontrolled can be life threatening. Even when not life-threatening, ketosis causes the loss of important minerals such as potassium, calcium, and magnesium.[54]

Heart Disease

The heart produces most of its energy from fats, and thus is dependent upon L-carnitine. An L-carnitine deficiency causes extreme metabolic impairment to heart tissue. On the other hand, supplemental L-carnitine has proved to be beneficial to heart patients. L-carnitine (20 or 40 mg/kg body weight) has increased the endurance of heart patients for exercise.[55] Other studies have shown that L-carnitine (40 mg/kg body weight) lowers the exercise heart rate, extends the time of exercise prior to the onset of angina, and at 100 mg/kg body weight, reduces the number of angina attacks and nitroglycerine consumption.[56]

Cirrhosis and Carnitine

Cirrhosis is a disease in which fibrous tissue displaces healthy liver tissue and liver functions are compromised. One of these functions happens to be the last step in the biochemical synthesis of carnitine, and people with cirrhosis show significant reductions in blood carnitine. In one study, when carnitine was given to rats fed on alcohol, the accumulation of fat in the liver was prevented and the blood lipid levels remained normal; at this time, it is not yet known whether the same applies to humans.[57]

Dietary Sources of L-Carnitine

Thee major sources of dietary L-carnitine are meat and dairy products. Vegetables, fruits, and cereals contain little or no L-carnitine.[58] All milks are rich in L-carnitine, and several studies suggest that L-carnitine is an essential nutrient for the newborn.[59]

TAURINE

The biological significance of taurine is now recognized by a growing number of nutritional and neurological researchers. There is strong evidence suggesting that this important amino acid is an essential dietary compound for humans and that deprivation of the newborn of a dietary source of taurine may have deleterious results. Taurine is needed for normal development and health of the central nervous system. Disturbances in taurine metabolism are seen in problems as diverse as epilepsy and heart disease.[60]

Taurine is a naturally occurring amino acid that does not occur in proteins.[61] Taurine is found in appreciable concentrations in the brain, and more taurine is found in the brain than in other tissues.[62] Taurine protects and stabilizes the brain's fragile membranes and acts as a neurotransmitter. Only in the last couple of years has taurine been added to the growing list of neurotransmitters. Taurine seems to be closely related in its structure and metabolism to other neurotransmitters such as glycine and GABA. Taurine, like GABA, is inhibitory.

Taurine, or a modified taurine, may someday supersede synthetic tranquilizers, but at this time further research is needed.[63] Antiseizure activity in epilepsy has been demonstrated with taurine intakes between 200 milligrams per day and 1500 milligrams per day, although intakes as high as 7000 milligrams have been used.[64]

Taurine also plays an important part in bile formation, and thus is important to fat metabolism and blood cholesterol control. This could prove very helpful in the alcoholic or sugar addict for fat metabolism and liver function.

In many mammals, taurine is synthesized from L-cysteine. However, in man, the bulk of the taurine is derived from dietary sources or produced from cysteine. An outstanding dietary source of taurine is animal/fish protein and marine animals, especially mollusca (oysters, clams, mussels, snails.)[65]

AMINO ACIDS AND THEIR EFFECT
ON THE BODY

Amino acid therapies are also making a great impact on general medicine. For example, amino acids in varying doses have been found to:

- Lower serum cholesterol and triglycerides:
  Arginine   Methionine
  Carnitine   Taurine
  Glycine

- Cause the release of growth hormone, prolactin, and other hormones:
  Arginine   Tryptophan
  Glycine   Valine
  Ornithine

- Build muscle tissue:
  Alanine   Isoleucine
  Carnitine   Valine
  Leucine

- Promote stamina
  Carnitine

- Help curb appetite:
  Arginine   Phenylalanine
  Carnitine   Tryptophan
  GABA   Tyrosine

- Help control hypoglycemia:
  Alanine   GABA

- Help control diabetes:
  Alanine   Tryptophan
  Cysteine

- Benefit liver disease patients:
  Isoleucine   Valine
  Leucine   Carnitine

- Reduce blood pressure:
  GABA   Tryptophan
  Taurine   Tyrosine with meals

- Relieve pain:
  Methionine   Tryptophan
  DLPA 750   Lysine-migraine headaches
  GABA-muscle tension

- Fight drug addiction:
  Amino Acids   *Drug*
  Methionine   Heroin
  Tyrosine   Cocaine
  Glutamine (GABA)   Alcohol

- Control Parkinson's disease:
  Tryptophan   Methionine
  Tyrosine   GABA
  L-Dopa   Threonine

- Relieve chorea and tardive dyskinesia:
  GABA   Leucine
  Isoleucine   Valine

- Help prevent insomnia:
  Tryptophan   Glycine
  GABA

- Provide relief for ailing gall bladders:
  Glycine   Methionine
  Isoleucine   Taurine
  Leucine   Valine

- Calm aggressiveness:
  Tryptophan   Taurine
  GABA   Glycine

The amino acid lysine may be useful in osteoporosis and some viral illnesses.

Through their metabolic pathways, amino acids have many roles in detoxification, and in building the immune system (immunostimulants):

Detoxification	Immunostimulants
Cysteine	Alanine
Glutamine	Aspartic Acid
Glycine	Cysteine
Methionine	Glycine
Taurine	Lysine
Tyrosine	Threonine

Some amino acids help the body resist the effects of radiation, which is becoming a significant pollutant and potentially a worldwide problem.[66]

DRUG-NUTRIENT INTER-ACTIONS[67]

DRUG	NUTRIENT WITH SIMILAR ACTION	NUTRIENT WITH ANTAGONISTIC ACTION
Antidepressants	Tyrosine Tryptophan Methionine	Glycine, Histidine
Anti-heart failure (inotropes)	Tyrosine, Taurine Carnitine	Niacin, Tryptophan
Anticonvulsants	Glycine, GABA Taurine, Alanine Tryptophan	Aspartic acid
Anabolic steroids	Branched chain amino acids, Alanine	Glutamic acid, Aspartic acid
Antivirals	Lysine, Zinc	Arginine
Antitoxins	Glycine, Cysteine	
Antipsychotics	Tryptophan, Isoleucine	Serine, Leucine
Antimanias	Glycine, Taurine Tryptophan	Methionine

AMINO ACIDS AND CLINICAL CONDITIONS AND DISEASES

Disease	Probable Therapy	To Be Avoided
Aging	Methionine, tryptophan	
Aggressiveness	Tryptophan	
Alzheimer's	All essential amino acids	
Appetite Control	Tryptophan, phenylalanine, GABA	
Arthritis	Histidine, cysteine	
Autism	Tryptophan	
Benign Prostatitis	Glycine	
Cancer	Cysteine, taurine, most essential amino acids	Phenylalanine Tyrosine
Cholesterol (elevated)	Methionine, taurine, glycine, carnitine, arginine	
Chronic Pain	Tryptophan, phenylalanine	
Cigarette Addiction	Tyrosine, GABA	
Cocaine Addiction	Tyrosine, GABA	
Depression	Tryptophan, methionine, phenylalanine, threonine, tyrosine	Arginine
Diabetes	Alanine, cysteine, tryptophan	
Drug Addiction	GABA, methionine, tyrosine	
Epilepsy	Glycine, taurine	Glutamic acid, aspartic acid
Gallbladder	Methionine, taurine, BCAA, glycine	
Gout	Glycine	

Disease	Probable Therapy	To Be Avoided
Hair Loss	Cysteine, arginine	
Heart Failure	Taurine, tyrosine, carnitine	
Herpes	Lysine	
Hypertension	Tryptophan, GABA, taurine, tyrosine with meals	
Hypoglycemia	Alanine, GABA	
Insomnia	Tryptophan	
Kidney Failure	Essential amino acids	Nonessential amino acids
Leg Ulcer	Topical cysteine, glycine threonine	
Liver Disease	Isoleucine, leucine, valine	
Manic Depression	Tryptophan, glycine	
Myasthenia	Glycine	
Osteoporosis	Lysine	
Parkinson's	Phenylalanine, tyrosine, tryptophan, methionine, L-Dopa	
Radiation Toxicity	Cysteine, taurine, methionine, glycine	
Schizophrenia	Isoleucine, tryptophan, methionine	Serine, asparagine, leucine[68]
Stress	Tyrosine, GABA histidine, all essential amino acids[69]	
Suicidal Depression	Tryptophan, methionine, tyrosine, phenylalanine	
Surgery	BCAA, all essential amino acids	
Thymus Insufficiency	Aspartic acid, threonine[70]	

SYMPTOMS OF VITAMIN DEFICIENCIES

THIAMINE (Vitamin B1)

Function: Builds resistance to infections, especially of the respiratory tract, helps maintain outer layers of tissues and organs, promotes growth and vitality, permits formation of visual purple of the eye, counteracts night blindness and weak eye sight, promotes healthy skin, essential for pregnancy and lactation.

Signs of Deficiency: Depression, chronic fatigue, apathy, appetite loss, irritability, memory loss, confusion, personality changes, aggression, anxiety, feelings of doom, lassitude, insomnia, restlessness, night tremors, noise sensitivity, indigestion, constipation, abdominal pains, nausea, vomiting, vague aches and pains, weak sore muscles, atrophy of leg muscles, heart palpitations, headaches, numbness and tingling or burning of feet and hands, circulation problems, shortness of breath, increased sensitivity to pain, weight loss.
Severe deficiency diseases: beriberi, polyneuritis, Wernicke-Korsakoff's syndrome.

Depleting or Risk Factors Alcohol, tobacco, excessive sugar, stress, white rice or flour, caffeine, raw clams and oysters, heavy exercise, pregnancy, lactation and nursing, aging, food processing and cooking, surgery, fever, sulfa drugs, birth control pills, hyperthyroidism.

Synergistic Nutrients B Complex, Vitamin C, Vitamin E, magnesium, manganese

Best Food Sources Wheat germ and bran, brewer's yeast, blackstrap molasses, organ meats, pork, soybeans, liver, nuts, oatmeal, peanuts, most vegetables, milk, poultry.

RIBOFLAVIN (Vitamin B2)

Function: Improves growth, essential for healthy eyes, skin and mouth, promotes general health.

Signs of Deficiency: Itching and burning eyes, cracking of the corners of the mouth, inflammation of the mouth, bloodshot eyes, purplish tongue, depression, mental sluggishness, dizziness, dermatitis, oily skin with scaling around nose, forehead, and ears, dry chapped lips, increased aging lines around the mouth, red sore tongue, crusty burning eyelids, sensitivity to lights, cataracts, trembling, vaginal itching, digestive disturbances, hair and eyebrow loss, tiny visible blood vessels on skin.

Depleting or Risk Factors: Stress, alcohol, excessive protein, excessive carbohydrates, excessive sugar, vegetarianism, pregnancy, nursing, high energy expenditures, liver disease, antibiotics, fever, exposure of food to sunlight, hyperthyroiditis.

Synergistic Nutrients: B Complex, Vitamin C, Iron, Vitamin A, copper, phosphorus.

Best Food Sources: Tongue, kidney, meat, fish, wheat germ, yeast, blackstrap molasses, beans, dairy products, nuts, green leafy vegetables, asparagus, currants, avocados.

NIACIN or NIACINAMIDE (Vitamin B3)

Function: Important for the proper functioning of nervous system, prevents pellegra, promotes growth, good mental attitude, maintains normal function of the gastrointestional tract and liver, necessary for normal brain function, needed for starch and sugar metabolism, needed for gums and mouth.

Signs of Deficiency: Mental fatigue, poor concentration, memory loss, nervous disorders, anxiety, fear, worry, apprehension, paranoia, irritability, insomnia, indigestion, gas, abdominal pains, nausea, diarrhea, sore mouth, painful swollen gums, halitosis, coated tongue but red-tipped, canker sores, muscle weakness, maladaptive behavior, skin eruptions, dermatitis, burning sensations anywhere on the body, weight loss, vague aches and pains, neuritis, general weakness.

Depleting or Risk Factors: Stress, caffeine, alcohol, corn, sugar, refined carbohydrates, antibiotics, illness, injury, physical exercise.

Synergistic Nutrients: B Complex, Vitamin C, phosphorus, tryptophan, adequate protein diet, chromium, zinc, Vitamin D.

Best Food Sources: Liver, rice bran, poultry, tuna, halibut, swordfish, peanuts, brewer's yeast, green leafy vegetables, beans, potatoes, nuts, grain, meats, mushrooms.

VITAMIN B5 (Pantothenic Acid)

Function: Helps in the building of body cells and maintaining normal skin, growth and development of central nervous system, required for snythesis of antibodies, necessary for normal digestive processes, believed to be important in color of hair, helpful in breaking down fatty acids.

Signs of Deficiency: Depression, quarrelsomeness, fatigue, weakness, restlessness, muscle cramps, diarrhea, dizzy spells, vomiting, sullenness, duodenal ulcers, eczema, allergies, hypoglycemia, poor wound healing, digestive disorders, constipation, arthritis, hair loss, skin ulcers, wrinkles, weight loss, premature aging, cramping in arms and legs, sore or burning feet, infection suscept-

*ibility with frequent respiratory illness, adrenal
insufficiency, low blood pressure, susceptibility
to infection.*

**Depleting
or Risk
Factors:**
Stress, tobacco, caffeine, illness, aging, injury,
sulfa drugs, estrogen, food processing.

**Synergistic
Nutrients:**
B Complex, Vitamin C, chromium, zinc.

**Best Food
Sources:**
Organ meats, liver, brewer's yeast, peanuts,
wheat bran and germ, eggs, herring, peas,
meats, salmon, clams, mackeral, walnuts,
whole grains, mushrooms, cheese, spinach,
brown rice, broccoli, cauliflower, carrots,
avocados.

VITAMIN B6 (Pyridoxine)

Function:
Assists in food assimilation, protein and fat
metabolism, helps to calm nerves, prevents nervous and skin disorders, important as a co-
factor in many body enzymatic reactions and in
activation of all amino acids.

**Signs of
Deficiency:**
Depression, irritability, insomnia, nervousness,
edema, dizziness, slow learning, poor dream
recall, premenstrual tension, increased sensitivity to sound, muscular weakness, poor
muscle tone, nausea, numbness and tingling in
limbs, carpal tunnel syndrome, neuritis, water
retention, decreased resistance to disease/infec-
tion, poor appetite, hair loss, cracks around
mouth and eyes, oily skin, acne, dermatitis,
dental cavities, low blood sugar and low
glucose tolerance, arthritis, anemia, convulsions, nervous disorders.

Depleting or Risk Factors: Stress, alcohol, birth control pills, tobacco, excessive sugar, pregnancy, nursing, exposure to radiation, high protein diet, food processing and cooking, Isoniazide (drug), Penicillamine (drug), heart failure.

Synergistic Nutrients: B Complex, Vitamin C, Vitamin E, magnesium, zinc, chromium, cobalt, sodium, potassium, copper, phosphorus, linoleic acid.

Best Food Sources: Liver, herring, blackstrap molasses, brewer's yeast, salmon, nuts, brown rice, meats, other fish, eggs, soybeans, butter, vegetables, bananas, avocados, grapes, pears.

VITAMIN B12 (Cobalamin)

Function: Helps in the formation and regeneration of red blood cells, helps to prevent pernicious anemia, helps with depression, decreased energy, and tiredness.

Signs of Deficiency: Mental apathy, depression, nervousness, general weakness, fatigue, poor memory and concentration, mood swings, intolerance to light and noise, confusion, sore tongue, loss of menstruation, disturbed digestion, numbness and tingling, hair loss, hallucinations, paranoia, psychosis, rapid heart beat, anemia, degeneration of the long nerve tracts in spinal cord, walking and speaking difficulties.

Depleting or Risk Factors: Stress, vegetarianism, alcohol, pregnancy, nursing, aging, estrogens, Dilantin (drug), excess Vitamin C, intestinal malabsorption and digestion problems, laxatives, loss of stomach "intrinsic factor," gastrectomy, cooking, hypothyroidism.

Synergistic Nutrients: B Complex vitamins with the exception of B3 or niacin, folic acid is especially helpful, calcium, iron, copper, phosphorus, Vitamin A, Vitamin

E, Vitamin C, choline, inositol, potassium, sodium.

Best Food Kidney, liver, brain, beef, pork, eggs, clams,
Sources: sardines, salmon, crabs, oysters, herring.

FOLIC ACID

Function: Essential to the formation of red blood cells by its action on the bone marrow, contributes to normal growth, important to liver function, important in reproductive glandular function.

Signs of Depression, mental lethargy, withdrawal, irri-
Deficiency: tability, sore tongue, poor memory, lesions at corners of the mouth, graying hair, increased sensitivity to pain, lowered resistance to infection, digestive disorders, diarrhea, low white blood cell count, anemia, toxemia, premature births, extreme lassitude and sleepiness, anxiety, hallucinations, grayish skin color, appetite loss, muscular pain, scaly dermatitis, dry skin, chest pain, slight anemia, hair loss.

Depleting Stress, alcohol, caffeine, birth control pills,
or Risk Methotrexate (drug), Aminopterin (drug),
Factors: Dilantin (drug), antibiotics, Phenobarbital (drug), pregnancy, nursing, food processing and cooking losses are great, illness, aging.

Synergistic B Complex, especially B12, Vitamin C, iron,
Nutrients: copper.

Best Food Liver, asparagus, spinach, brewer's yeast, dry
Sources: beans (lentils, lima, navy), green vegetables, almonds, filberts, peanuts, walnuts, oats, rye, wheat.

BIOTIN

Function: Important in amino acid synthesis, tears, saliva production, normal growth.

Signs of Deficiency: Depression, extreme lassitude and sleepiness, anxiety, hallucinations, grayish skin color, appetite loss, muscular pain, scaly dermititis, dry skin, chest pain, slight anemia, hair loss.

Depleting or Risk Factors: Stress, avidin (in raw egg whites), antibiotics.

Synergistic Nutrients: B Complex, manganese, Vitamin C.

Best Food Sources: Brewer's yeast, royal bee jelly, liver, wheat, brown rice, chick peas, corn, lentils, oats, soybeans, barley, eggs, chicken, mushrooms, nuts, mackerel, salmon, sardines.

CALCIUM

Function: Builds and maintains bones and teeth, helps with blood clotting, important to heart and muscle contraction, helps to calm nerves, important to mental health.

Signs of Deficiency: Muscular cramping and convulsions, osteoporosis, osteomalacia, brittle bones.

Depleting or Risk Factors: Stress, low stomach acid.

Synergistic Nutrients: Calcium, phosphorus, zinc, Vitamin D. Calcium must be in balance with phosphorus at 2:1 ratio

Best Food Sources: Dairy products, broccoli.

MAGNESIUM

Function: Essential for normal functioning of nervous and muscular system, important in enzymatic reactions in the body, aids in utilization of Vitamins C and E.

Signs of Deficiency: Fatigue, anxiety, insomnia, nervousness, depression, confusion, hyperactivity, disorientation, learning disability, easily aroused anger, increased sensitivity to noise and startled response, tremors, muscle twitching, numbness and tingling, appetite loss, rapid pulse, heart irregularities, kidney stones, high blood pressure.

Depleting or Risk Factors: Alcohol, aging, excessive sugar, cooking in water, low protein diet, long-term dieting, irradiation, soil deficiencies, birth control pills, excess protein, fat, calcium, and Vitamin D, diuretics, burns, surgery.

Synergistic Nutrients: Vitamin B6, Vitamin C, Vitamin D, potassium, calcium, phosphorus, protein.

Best Food Sources: Wheat germ and bran, almonds, Brazil nuts, blackstrap molasses, cashews, brewer's yeast, nuts, soybeans, sesame seeds, parsnips, wild rice, oats, rye, mullet, barley, corn, peas, carrots, beet greens, sunflower seeds, figs.

ZINC

Function: Important to immune system and wound healing, needed for male hormones and prostate health, necessary for brain amine formation, involved in multiple physiological functions.

Signs of Deficiency: Loss of sense of taste and smell, apathy, fatigue, poor dream recall, appetite loss, oily skin, prolonged wound healing, stretch marks on the skin, failure of growth, brittle nails, white spots on nails, poor hair growth, acne, menstrual irregularities, prostate disorders, painful knees and hips especially in children and teenagers, cold extremities with poor circulation.

Depleting or Risk Factors: Stress, alcohol, excess calcium intake, excess copper intake, pregnancy, nursing, surgery, burns, food processing, high phytate diet, birth control pills, excess iron, estrogen intake.

Synergistic Nutrients: Vitamin B6, Vitamin E, Vitamin A, calcium.

Best Food Sources: Liver, oysters, herring, sunflower seeds, pumpkin seeds, cheese, wheat germ and bran, seafood, meats, peanuts, cashews, other grains, avocados, vegetables.

IRON

Function: Necessary for formation of red blood cells and carrying of oxygen in the body.

Signs of Deficiency: Fatigue, listlessness, depression, impaired learning, poor memory and attention span, headaches, irritability, dizziness, weakness, sore or burning tongue, brittle, flattened or spoon-shaped nails, longitudinal ridges in nails, constipation, heart palpitations on exertion, shortness of breath, difficulty in swallowing, cold extremities, decreased resistance to infection, anemia, numbness and tingling.

Depleting or Risk Factors Vegetarianism, caffeine, excessive zinc, calcium or phosphorus, aging, illness, copper deficiency, pregnancy, lactation and nursing, antacid use, boiling food, high phytate diet, tetracyclines (drug).

Synergistic Nutrients: Vitamin C, Vitamin E, Vitamin B12, folic acid, calcium, copper, amino acids, alcohol.

Best Food Sources: Blackstrap molasses, liver, brewer's yeast, kidneys, clams, caviar, seeds—sesame, sunflower, and pumpkin, walnuts, almonds, pistachio, pine nuts, millet, soybeans, parsley, wheat germ and bran, brown rice, seafood, meats, vegetables, cheese, raisins.[71]

VITAMIN A

Function: Needed for vision, strong mucous membranes, healthy reproduction and lactation, reduces susceptibility to infection, needed for good appetite and digestion.

Signs of Deficiency: Emaciation, poor or reduced vision, dry skin and acne, digestive disturbances, colds and membrane infection, diarrhea, night blindness.

Best Food Sources: Yellow vegetables, pumpkin, butternut squash, green leafy vegetables, carrots, apricots, liver, fish liver oil, parsley.

VITAMIN E

Function: Important anti-oxidant, needed for healthy heart and blood vessels, important to circulation, needed for production of hormones.

Signs of Deficiency: Aging, infections, infertility, increased fragility of red blood cells, muscular disorders.

Best Food Sources: Wheat germ, rice bran, soybeans, peanut oil, corn oil, whole wheat, green leafy vegetables, meat, eggs.

DIETARY PRECURSORS AND EFFECTS[72]

Dietary Precursor	Biochemical Involved in the body	Effect
L-Phenylalanine	Phenyethylamine	Antidepressant
L-Tyrosine	Dopamine	Mental Alertness Sedative Diuretic Anorexia
	Norepinephrine (Noradrenalin)	Aggressiveness Drive Euphoria or feeling high
	Epinephrine (Adrenalin)	Anxiety
L-Tryptophan	Serotonin	Tension Drowsiness Inability to concentrate Antidiuretic Tachycardia or pulse greater than 100
L-Glutamine	Gamma Amino Butyric Acid	Sedation Anticonvulsant
Choline	Acetylcholine	Memory Coordination

Footnotes

CHAPTER I   What Is Drug Addiction?

[1]Kenneth Blum, *Handbook of Abusable Drugs* (New York: Gardner Press, Inc., 1984), p. 5.

[2]Ibid.

[3]Roy W. Pickens and Leonard L. Heston, eds., *Psychiatric Factors in Drug Abuse* (New York: Grune and Stratton, Inc., 1979). pp. 1-238.

[4]Janice Phelps and Alan E. Nourse, *The Hidden Addiction and How to Get Free* (Boston: Little, Brown and Co., 1986), pp. 35-41.

[5]R.C. Garrett and U.G. Waldmeyer, *The Pill Book of Anxiety and Depression* (New York: Bantam Books, 1985), p. 9.

[6]Phelps and Nourse, loc cit.

[7]Max Ricketts with Edwin Bien, *The Great Anxiety Escape Guidebook*. In preparation.

[8]Ibid.

[9]Billie J. Sahley, *The Anxiety Epidemic* (San Antonio: Watercress Press, 1986), pp. 39-48.

[10]Ricketts with Bien, op. cit.

[11]Ibid.

[12]Blum, op. cit.

CHAPTER II Withdrawal and Recovery

[1]Shirley Trickett, *Coming Off Tranquilizers* (New York: Ballantine Books, 1984), p. 100.

[2]Phyllis Saifer and Merla Zellerbach, *Detox* (New York: Ballantine Books, 1984), p. 100.

[3]Ibid pp. 97-98.

[4]Trickett, op. cit., p. 30.

[5]Saifer and Zellerbach, op. cit., pp. 101-105.

[6]Kenneth Blum, *Handbook of Abusable Drugs* (New York: Gardner Press, Inc., 1984), p. 205.

[7]Trickett, op. cit., pp. 29-30.

[8]Michael C. Gerald, *Pharmacology, An Introduction to Drugs* (New York: Prentice-Hall, 1981), pp. 30-31.

[9]Eric Braverman and Carl C. Pfeiffer, *The Healing Nutrients Within: Facts, Findings and New Research on Amino Acids* (New Canaan, CN: Keats Publishing Co., Inc., 1987), p. 8.

[10]Billie J. Sahley, *The Anxiety Epidemic* (San Antonio: The Watercress Press, 1986), p. 7.

[11]Trickett, op. cit., pp. 29-30.

[12]Ibid., pp. 30-39.

CHAPTER III Alcoholism and its Treatment

[1]James R. Milam and Katherine Kethcám, *Under the Influence* (New York: Bantam Books, 1983), p. 31-37.

[2]Lendon Smith, *Feed Yourself Right* (New York: Dell Publishing Co., 1983), p. 108.

³Milam, op. cit., p. 33.

⁴Myron Brenton and Editors of Prevention Magazine, *Emotional Health* (Emmaus, PA: Rodale Press, 1985), p. 129.

⁵Smith, op. cit., p. 33.

⁶Richard I. Shader, ed., *Manual of Psychiatric Therapeutics* (Boston: Little, Brown, and Co., 1984), p. 273.

⁷Ibid., p. 289.

⁸Ibid., p. 213.

⁹Milam, op. cit., pp. 36-38.

¹⁰Ibid., op. cit., pp. 34.

¹¹Robert S. Goodhart and Maurice E. Shils, *Modern Nutrition in Health and Disease* (Philadelphia: Lea & Febiger, 1980), pp. 1220-1221.

¹²Daphne A. Roe, *Drug-Induced Nutritional Deficiencies* (Westport, CN: Avi Publishing Co., 1978), pp. 200-201.

¹³Ibid., loc. cit., p. 207.

¹⁴Durk Pearson and Sandy Shaw, *Alcohol* (Huntington Beach, CA: International Institute of Natural Health Sciences, Inc., 1981), p. 20.

¹⁵Goodhart and Shils, loc. cit.

¹⁶Pearson and Shaw, op. cit., pp. 20-21.

¹⁷Goodhart and Shils, loc. cit.

¹⁸Roe, p. 208.

¹⁹Roe, loc. cit., pp. 204-208.

²⁰Smith, loc. cit., pp. 112

²¹Carl C. Pfeiffer, *Mental and Elemental Nutrients* (New Canaan, CN: Keats Publishing Co., 1975), pp. 382-383.

CHAPTER IV Nicotine and Caffeine Addiction and Treatment

[1]Brian Leibovitz, *Carnitine, The Vitamin B*$_T$ *Phenomenon* (New York: Dell Books, 1984), p. 1318.

[2]Phyllis Saifer and Merla Zellerbach, *Detox* (New York: Ballantine Books, 1984), p. 135.

[3]Priscilla Slagle, *The Way Up From Down* (New York: St. Martin's Press), p. 149.

[4]Leibovitz, op. cit., pp. 1318-29.

[5]Saifer and Zellerbach, op. cit., pp. 136-37.

[6]Slagle, op. cit., 142-43.

[7]Ibid., p. 113.

[8]Ibid., pp. 142-45.

[9]Saifer and Zellerbach, op. cit., p. 113.

[10]Slagle, op. cit., pp. 144-45.

CHAPTER V Amino Acids For Therapy

[1]W.B. Essman, ed., *Nutrients and Brain Function* (Switzerland: S. Karger, 1987), pp. 2-3.

[2]Richard Bergland, *The Fabric of the Mind* (New York: Viking Penguin, Inc., 1985), pp. 80-98.

[3]Billie J. Sahley, *The Anxiety Epidemic* (San Antonio, TX: The Watercress Press, 1986), pp. 19-27.

[4]Malcolm Lader, *Introductions to Psychopharmacology* (Kalamazoo, MI: The Upjohn Co., 1983), pp. 99-100.

[5]Harold A. Harper, *Review of Physiological Chemistry* (Los Altos, CA: Lange Medical Publications, 1969), p. 275.

[6]J.M. Ravel, et al., "Reversal of Alcohol Toxicity by Glutamine," *The Journal of Biological Chemistry*, 214 (1955), pp. 497-501.

[7]L.L. Rogers, R.B. Pelton, and R. Williams, "Voluntary Alcohol Consumption Following Administration of Glutamine," *The Journal of Biological Chemistry*, 214 (1955), pp. 503-506.

[8]L.L. Rogers, R.B. Pelton, and R. Williams, "Amino Acid Supplementation and Voluntary Alcohol Consumption by Rats," *The Journal of Biological Chemistry*, 220, (1955), pp. 321-23.

[9]R.J. Williams, *Alcoholism: The Nutritional Approach* (Austin, TX: University of Texas Press, 1958), p. 88.

[10]J.B. Trunnell and J.I. Wheeler, "Preliminary Report on Experiments with Orally Administered Glutamine in Treatment of Alcoholics," *American Chemistry Society Meeting Notes* (Houston, TX: December, 1955).

[11]L.L. Rogers, "Glutamine in the Treatment of Alcoholism," *Quarterly Journal of Studies on Alcohol*, 18 (1957), pp. 581-87.

[12]W. Shive, et al., "Glutamine in Treatment of Peptic Ulcer," *Texas State Journal of Medicine*, 53 (1957), pp. 840-43.

[13]H.L. Newbold, *Mega-Nutrients for Your Nerves* (New York: Peter Wyden Publishing, 1975).

[14]R.J. Williams and E.M. Lansford, *The Encyclopedia of Biochemistry* (New York: Reinhold, 1967), p. 375.

[15]A. Hoffer, *Orthomolecular Psychiatry*, D. Hawkins and L. Pauling, eds. (San Francisco: Freeman and Co., 1973), p. 238.

[16]Williams, *Alcoholism: The Nutritional Approach*, op. cit., p. 375.

[17]R.J. Williams, *Nutrition Against Disease* (New York: Pitman Publishing Corp., 1971), p. 178.

[18]Newbold, op. cit.

[19]Larry A. Grant, "Amino Acids in Action," *Let's Live* (August, 1983), p. 63.

[20]Eric Braverman and Carl C. Pfeiffer, *The Healing Nutrients Within: Facts, Findings and New Research on Amino Acids* (New Canaan, CN: Keats Publishing Co., Inc., 1982), pp. 29-58

[21]Robert Garrison, Jr., *Lysine, Tryptophan, and Other Amino Acids* (New Canaan, CN: Keats Publishing Co., Inc., 1982), pp. 2-9.

[22]Bernard H. Smith and Antonio Rosich-Pla, "The Biochemistry of Mental Illness," *Psychosomatics* (April, 1979), p. 279.

[23]Michael Bond, *Pain, Its Nature, Analysis, and Treatment* (New York: Churchill Livingstone, 1979), p. 102.

[24]B. Smith and Rosich-Pla, op. cit., p. 282.

[25]Ibid.

[26]Garrison, op. cit., pp. 7-8.

[27]Arnold Fox and Barry Fox, *DLPA, To End Chronic Pain and Depression* (New York: Pocket Books, 1985), pp. 147-199.

[28]Kenneth Blum and Michael C. Trachtenberg, *Some Things You Should Know About Alcoholism* (Houston, TX: MATRIX Technologies, Inc., 1988).

[29]Fox and Fox, loc. cit.

[30]Stein, et al., "Memory Enhancement by Central Administration of Norepinephrine," *Brain Research,* 84 (1975), pp. 329-35.

[31]R. Partridge, "Regulation of Amino Acid Availability to the Brain," *Nutrition and the Brain*, Wurtman and Wurtman, ed. (New York: Raven Press, 1979), pp. 141-204.

[32]A. Growden, "Neurotransmitter Precursors in the Diet," *Nutrition and the Brain*, Wurtman and Wurtman, eds. (New York: Raven Press, 1979), pp. 117-81.

[33]Alan J. Gelenberg, et al., "Tyrosine for the Treatment of Depression," *American Journal of Psychiatry* (May, 1980), pp. 622-623.

³⁴A. White, et al., *Principles of Biochemistry* (New York: McGraw-Hill, 1978), pp. 1241-64.

³⁵David E. Bresler with Richard Trubo, *Free Yourself From Pain* (New York: Simon and Schuster, 1979), p. 298.

³⁶Alan Gaby, *B-6, The Healing Nutrient* (New Canaan, CN: Keats Publishing, Inc., 1984), pp. 58-62.

³⁷Jack E. Booker, "Pain It's All in Your Patient's Head (Or Is It?)," *Nursing 82*, March, pp. 47-51.

³⁸Braverman and Pfeiffer, op. cit.

³⁹Schneider-Helmert Dietrich, Interval Therapy with L-Tryptophan in Severe Chronic Insomniacs," *International Pharmacopsychiatry*, 16 (1981), pp. 162-173.

⁴⁰Bresler with Turbo, op. cit., p. 67.

⁴¹Robert B. King, "Pain and Tryptophan," *Journal Neurosurgery,* 53 (July, 1980), pp. 48-50.

⁴²Bresler with Turbo, op. cit.

⁴³*New Frontiers in Pain Control: Alternatives to Drugs and Surgery* (Pacific Palisades, CA: Center for Intergral Medicine, 1978), p. 20.

⁴⁴Bresler with Turbo, op. cit.

⁴⁵Jeffrey Bland, *Medical Applications of Clinical Nutrition* (New Canaan, CN: Keats Publishing, Inc., 1983).

⁴⁶Joseph Fruton and Sofia Simmonds, *General Biochemistry* (New York: Wiley, 1958), p. 792.

⁴⁷G. Colombetti and S. Monti, *European Physiology Congress Proceedings,* 1st Qtr., No. 2 (1971), p. 45-53.

⁴⁸Fruton and Simmonds, loc. cit.

⁴⁹D. Pearson and R. Shaffer, *Nutritional Consultants* (November-December), 1980), p. 12.

⁵⁰Colombetti and Monti, loc. cit.

108 / BREAKING YOUR ADDICTION HABIT

⁵¹K. Khaleeluddin and W. Philpott, "Data Sheet," (Oklahoma City, OK: Philpott Medical Center, 1980).

⁵²Brian Leibovitz, *Carnitine, The Vitamin Bт Phenomenon* (New York: Peter Wyden Publications, 1975) Reprint, New York: Dell Books, 1984.

⁵³Janice Phelps and Alan E, Nourse, *The Hidden Addiction and How to Get Free* (Boston: Little, Brown and Co., 1986), pp. 79-85.

⁵⁴Leibovitz, op. cit.

⁵⁵A. Cherchi, et al., *American Journal of Cardiology* Vol. 33 (1979), pp. 300-306.

⁵⁶G. Garzya and R.M. Amico, *International Journal Tissue Reactions,* 11 (1980), pp. 175-80.

⁵⁷Braverman and Pfeiffer, op. cit., pp. 306-14.

⁵⁸P.R. Borum, *Annual Review Nutrition,* 3 (1983), pp. 233-59.

⁵⁹P.R. Borum, *Nutrition Review,* 39 (1981), pp. 285-390.

⁶⁰R.J. Huxtable and H. Pasantes-Morales, *Taurine in Nutrition and Neurology* (New York: Plenum Press, 1981).

⁶¹Harper, op. cit., p. 29.

⁶²A. White, et al., op. cit., p. 1120.

⁶³Braverman and Pfeiffer, op. cit., p. 124.

⁶⁴A. Barbeau, *Archives Neurology,* 30 (1982), pp. 52-58.

⁶⁵Braverman and Pfeiffer, op. cit., pp. 120-127.

⁶⁶Braverman and Pfeiffer, op. cit., pp. 12-13.

⁶⁷Braverman and Pfeiffer, op. cit., p. 24.

⁶⁸Braverman and Pfeiffer, op. cit., p. 330-331.

⁶⁹Sahley, op. cit., pp. 21-27.

[70]Braverman and Pfeiffer, op. cit., p. 331.

[71]Slagle, op. cit., pp. 241-247.

[72]W.B. Essman, ed., *Nutrients and Brain Function* (Switzerland: Karger, 1987), p. 164.

Bibliography

Adams, Ruth and Frank Murray. *Megavitamin Therapy*. New York: Larchmont Books, 1980.

Adour, K., R. Hilsinger, and F. Byl. *American Otolaryngology Annual Meeting Review Notes*. Dallas, Texas. October 7-11, 1985.

Barbeau, A. *Archives Neurology*. Vol. 30 (1982).

Beckmann, H., D. Athen, M. Oheanu, and R. Zimmer. "DL-phenylalanine Versus Imipramine: A Double Blind Controlled Study." *Archives Psychiatric Nervenkr*. Vol. 227 (1979).

Benowitz, Neal L. "Pharmacologic Aspects of Cigarette Smoking and Nicotine Addiction." *The New England Journal of Medicine*. (Nov. 17, 1988.)

Bergland, Richard. *The Fabric of the Mind*. New York: Viking Penguin, Inc., 1985.

Berman, J.R. "Progabide, A New GABA Mimetric Agent in Clinical Use." *Clinical Neuropharmacology*. (1985.)

Blum, Kenneth. *Handbook of Abusable Drugs*. New York: Gardner Press, Inc., 1984.

Blum, Kenneth and Michael C. Trachtenberg. *Some Things You Should Know About Alcoholism*. Houston, Texas: MATRIX Technologies, Inc., 1988

Bond, Michael. *Pain, Its Nature, Analysis, and Treatment.* New York: Churchill Livingstone, 1979.

Booker, Jack E. "Pain It's All in Your Patient's Head (Or is It?)," *Nursing 82.* March.

Borison, et al. "Metabolism of the Antidepressant Amino Acid, L-phenylalanine." *Fellows of American Society of Experimental Biology Meeting Notes.* April 9-14, 1978.

Borum, P.R. *Annual Review Nutrition.* Vol. 3 (1983).
-----*Nutrition Review.* Vol. 39 (1981).

Braverman, Eric R. and Carl C. Pfeiffer. *The Healing Nutrients Within: Facts, Findings and the New Research on Amino Acids.* New Canaan, Connecticut: Keats Publishing Co., Inc., 1987.

Brenton, Myron and eds. *Emotional Health.* Emmaus, PA: Rodale Press, 1985.

Bresler, David E. with Richard Trubo. *Free Yourself From Pain.* New York: Simon and Schuster, 1979.

Chaitow, Leon. *Amino Acids in Therapy.* Rochester, Vermont: Thorsons Publishers, Inc., 1985.

Cherchi, A. et al. *American Journal of Cardiology.* Vol. 33 (1979).

Colombetti, G. and S. Monti. *European Physiology Congress Proceedings.* 1st Quarter, No. 2. 1971.

Devlin, T.M. *Textbook of Biochemistry.* New York: Wiley Press, 1982.

Diamond, Seymour and Jose Medina. "Headaches." *Clinical Symposia.* Vol. 33, No. 2 (1981).

Essman, W.B., ed. *Nutrients and Brain Function.* Switzerland: Karger, 1987.

Feldberg and Hetzel. *Food Technology.* Vol. 12 (1958).

Fischer, E., B. Heller, and N. Miro. "Beta-phenylethylamine Human Urine." *Arzneim-Forsch.* Vol. 18 (1958).

Fischer, E., H. Spatz, J.M. Saaverdra, H. Reggiani, A.H. Miro, and B. Heller. "Urinary Elimination of Phenylethylamine." *Biological Psychiatry.* Vol. 2, No. 2 (1972).

Fox, Arnold and Barry Fox. *DLPA, To End Chronic Pain and Depression.* New York: Pocket Books, 1985.

Fruton, Joseph and Sofia Simmonds. *General Biochemistry.* New York: Wiley, 1958.

Gaby, Alan. *B-6, The Healing Nutrient.* New Canaan, CN: Keats Publishing, Inc., 1984.

Galton, Lawrence. *Parade.* (29 July, 1979.)

Garrett, R.C. and U.G. Waldmeyer. *The Pill Book of Anxiety and Depression.* New York: Bantam Books, 1985.

Garrison, Robert Jr. *Lysine, Tryptophan, and Other Amino Acids.* New Canaan, Connecticut: Keats Publishing, Co., Inc., 1982.

Garzya, G. and R.M. Amico. *International Journal Tissue Reactions.* Vol. 11 (1980).

Gelenberg, Alan J et al. "Tyrosine for the Treatment of Depression." *American Journal of Psychiatry.* (May 1980).

Gerald, Michael C. *Pharmacology, An Introduction to Drugs* New York: Prentice-Hall, 1981.

Gerber, D.A. "Low Free Serum Histidine Concentration in Rheumatoid Arthritis." *Clinical Investigations.* Vol. 55 (1975).

Gerber, Harris, and Frizzel. "Treatment of Rheumatoid Arthritis with Histidine—A Double Blind Trial." *Arthritis and Rheumatism.* (Jan.-Feb. 1973).

Gerner, H., D.A. Gorelick, D.H. Catlin, and C.H. Li. "Behavioral Effects of Beta-endorphin in Depression and Schizophrenia." *Endorphins and Opiate Antagonists in Psychiatric Research, Clinical Implications.* New York: Plenum Press, 1982.

Goldberg, I. "Tyrosine in Depression." *Lancet.* August 1980.

Goodheart, Robert S. and Maurice E. Shils. *Modern Nutrition in Health and Disease.* Philadelphia: Lea & Febiger, 1980.

Grant, Larry A. "Amino Acids in Action." *Let's Live.* (August, 1983).

Greenstein, J.F. and M. Winitz. *Chemistry of the Amino Acids.* New York: Wiley Press, 1961.

Growden, A., Wurtman and Wurtman, eds. "Neurotransmitter Precursors in the Diet." *Nutrition and the Brain.* New York: Raven Press, 1979.

Harper, Harold A. *Review of Physiological Chemistry.* Los Altos, California: Lange Medical Publications, 1969.

Heller, B. "Pharmacological and Clinical Effects of D-phenylalanine in Depression and Parkinson's Disease." *Modern Pharmacology-Toxicology.* (1985.)

Hoffer, Abram. *Orthomolecular Nutrition.* New Canaan, Connecticut: Keats Publishing, Inc., 1978.

Huxtable, R.J., and H. Pasantes-Morales. *Taurine in Nutrition and Neurology.* New York: Plenum Press, 1981.

Kagan, C., R. Griffith, and A. Norins. *Dermatologica.* Vol. 156. (1978).

Khaleeluddin, K. and W. Philpott. "Data Sheet." Philpott Medical Center, Oklahoma City, Oklahoma, (1980.)

Lader, Malcolm. *Introduction to Psychopharmacology.* Kalamazoo, Michigan: The Upjohn Co., 1983.

Lapedes, Daniel. *Encyclopedia of Food, Agriculture and Nutrition.* New York: McGraw-Hill, 1977.

Leibovitz, Brian. *Carnitine, The Vitamin B$_T$ Phenomenon.* New York: Dell Books, 1984.

Meister, A. *Biochemistry of the Amino Acids.* New York: Academic Press, 1975.

Milam, James R. and Katherine Kethcam. *Under the Influence*. New York: Bantam Books, 1983.

Newbold, H.L. *Mega-Nutrients for Your Nerves*. New York: Peter Wyden Publishing, 1975.

Partridge, R., Wurtman and Wurtman, eds. "Regulation of Amino Acid Availability to the Brain." *Nutrition and the Brain*. New York: Raven Press, 1977.

Pauling, Linus. *Orthomolecular Psychiatry*. San Francisco: Freeman and Co., 1973.

Pearson, D., and R. Shaffer. *Nutritional Consultants*. (November - December, 1980).

Pearson, Durk and Sandy Shaw. *Alcohol*. Huntington Beach, California: International Institute of Natural Health Sciences, Inc., 1981.

Pfeiffer, Carl C. *Mental and Elemental Nutrients*. New Canaan, Connecticut: Keats Publishing Co., 1975.

Phelps, Janice and Alan E. Nourse. *The Hidden Addiction and How to Get Free*. Boston: Little, Brown and Co., 1986.

Pickens, Roy W. and Leonard L. Heston, eds. *Psychiatrics Factors in Drug Abuse*. New York: Grune & Stratton, 1979.

Pickup, Dixon, Lowe, and Wright. "Serum Histidine in Rheumatoid Arthritis: Changes Introduced by Antirheumatic Drug Therapy." *The Journal of Rheumatology*. Vol. 17, No. 1 (1980).

Rapp, Doris J. *Allergies and the Hyperactive Child*. New York: Simon and Schuster, Inc., 1979.
-----*Allergies and Your Family*. Buffalo, New York: Practical Allergy Research Foundation, 2nd edition, 1990.

Ravel, J.M., B. Felsing, E.M. Lansford, R.H. Trubey, and W. Shive. "Reversal of Alcohol Toxicity by Glutamine." *The Journal of Biological Chemistry*. Vol. 214, No. 2 (1955).

Ricketts, Max, with Edward Bien. *The Great Anxiety Escape Guidebook.* In preparation.

Roe, Daphne A. *Drug-Induced Nutritional Deficiencies.* Westport, Connecticut: Avi Publishing Co., 1978.

Rogers, L.L. "Glutamine in the Treatment of Alcoholism." *Quarterly Journal of Studies on Alcohol.* Vol. 18, No. 4 (1957).

Rogers, L.L., R.B. Pelton. "Effect of Glutamine on IQ Scores of Mentally Deficient Children." *Texas Reports on Biology and Medicine.* Vol. 15, No. 1 (1957)

Rogers, L.L., R.B. Pelton, and R. Williams. "Voluntary Alcohol Consumption Following Administration of Glutamine." *The Journal of Biological Chemistry.* Vol. 214, No. 2 (1955).
-----."Amino Acid Supplementation and Voluntary Alcohol Consumption by Rats." *The Journal of Biological Chemistry.* Vol. 220, No. 1 (1956).

Rose, W.C., D.E. Leach, J.J. Coon, and G.F. Lamberg. "The Amino Acid Requirements of Man. The Phenylalanine Requirement." *The Journal of Biological Chemistry.* Vol. 213 (1955).

Sabelli, H and A.D. Mosnaim. "Phenylethlamine Hypothesis of Affective Behavior." *American Journal of Psychiatry* Vol. 131 (1974).

Sahley, Billie J. *The Anxiety Epidemic.* San Antonio, Texas: The Watercress Press, 1986.

Saifer, Phyllis and Merla Zellerbach. *Detox.* New York: Ballantine Books, 1984.

Shader, Richard I., ed. *Manual of Psychiatric Therapeutics.* Boston: Little, Brown, and Co., 1984.
-----*Brain.* New York: Raven Press, 1979.

Shive, W., et al. "Glutamine in Treatment of Peptic Ulcer." *Texas State Journal of Medicine.* Vol. 53 (1957).

Slagle, Priscilla. *The Way Up From Down.* New York: St. Martin's Press, 1987.

116 / BREAKING YOUR ADDICTION HABIT

Smith, Bernard H. and Antonio Rosich-Pla. "The Biochemistry of Mental Illness." *Psychosomatics*. (April, 1979).

Smith, Lendon. *Feed Yourself Right*. New York: Dell Publishing Co., Inc., 1983.

Spatz, H., B. Heller, M. Nachon, and E. Fischer. "Effects of D-phenylalanine on Clinical Picture and Phenylethylaminuria in Depression." *Biological Psychiatry*. Vol. 10, No. 2 (1975).

Stein, et al. "Memory Enhancement by Central Administration of Norepinephrine." *Brain Research*. Vol. 84 (1975).

Trickett, Shirley. *Coming Off Tranquilizers*. New York: Thorson Publishing Group. 1986.

Trunnell, J.B. and J.I. Wheeler. "Preliminary Report on Experiments with Orally Administered Glutamine in Treatment of Alcoholics." *American Chemistry Society Meeting Notes*. Houston, Texas. (December, 1955).

White, A., et al. *Principles of Biochemistry*. New York: McGraw-Hill, 1978.

Williams, R.J. *Encyclopedia of Biochemistry*. New York: Reinhold, 1967.
-----.*Alcoholism: The Nutritional Approach*. Austin: University of Texas Press, 1958.
-----.*Nutrition Against Disease*. New York: Pitman Publishing Corporation, 1971.

Wurtman, Carl and Judith Wurtman, eds. *Nutrition and the Brain*. New York: Raven Press, 1979.

Index

Ascorbic acid, 43
Acetylcholine, 47
ACTH, 47
Addiction, 9, 15
Addictive personality, 7
Adrenalin, 54
Alcohol, 12, 34
  as MAO inhibitor, 36
  and cystine,
  calories, 41
  metabolism, 38
Alcoholism, 34-35, 39
  and malnutrition, 40-41
  and nutritional deficiencies,
  42
  therapeutic treatment of,
  44-45
Alcohol withdrawal, 36-37
  early, 36-37
  late, 37
  severe, 37
Allergic reactions, 32-33
Amino acids, effect on
  body, 55-56
  and disease, 53-89
Amphetamines, 14
Angel dust, 14
Anxiety, 20, 25, 28, 56
  rebound, 25-29

Ativan, 10, 23

BAM, 17
Barbiturates, 13
B Complex, 16, 29, 44, 45
B5, 47
B6, 20, 42, 43, 47, 55, 62, 76,
  81
B12, 42, 43
Benzodiazepines, 11, 22
Beta-carotene, 29
Bipolar depression, 65
Blood-brain barrier, 47, 75,
  78
Branch chain amino acids
  (BCAA), 17, 55-56

Caffeine, 49, 50-52
  detox procedure, 51
  substance content, 50
Calcium, 43, 44
Carnitine, 81-83
  and cirrhosis, 83
  and fats, 82
  and heart disease, 82
  dietary sources, 83
Catecholamines, 54, 65
Choline, 54

Circadian rhythms, 78
Cocaine, 14, 75
Corticoid sclerosis, 42
Cysteine, 47, 79-81

Depression, 65, 67, 68, 72, 76
    treatment, 68-72
Dietary precursors, 100
DLPA, 17, 44, 45, 66-73, 75
DL-phenylalanine, 17, 44,
    45, 66-73, 75
Dopa, 63, 73
Dopamine, 15, 47, 53, 63,
    73, 74
Drinking symptoms,
    progression, 35
Drug nutrient interactions, 87
Drug-induced nutritional
    deficiencies, 42

Endorphins, 69-70
Enkephalins, 70
Epilepsy, 61
Epinephrine, 63, 73, 74
Esterified C, 16, 20, 31-32
    44, 49, 52

Folic Acid, 42, 43

GABA, 16, 20, 29, 49, 52
    53, 56-58, 75, 76
Genetic depression, 8-9
Ginkgo Biloba, 17
Ginseng, 29
Glutamine, 16, 20, 44,
    59-62, 75
Glutathione, 80
Glycine, 54
Grief reactions, 26-27
Growth hormone, 47
Gymnema Sylvestre, 17

Halcion, 10, 23
Hallucinogens, 14
Heroin, 13, 70
Histamine, 53
Hormones, 47
Hydrochloric acid, 49

Hyperactivity, 8-9, 23, 32-33
    76
Hypoglycemia, 43, 60, 82

Inhalants, 13
Imipramine, 71
Isoleucine, 55, 77
Isoquinolines, 39
Iron, 51, 81

Korsakoff's syndrome, 42
Ketosis, 82

L-Carnitine, 81-83
L-Cystine, 79-81
Leucine, 54, 55, 77
Librax, 11
Librium, 10
Loxitane, 11
LSD, 14
Lysine, 20, 81

Magnesium, 29, 42, 43, 44
MAO, 65
MAO inhibitor, 36, 66
Marijuana, 13
Metabolism of alcohol, 38
Methadone, 13
Methionine, 20, 54, 79, 81
Minor tranquilizers, 14
Morel's corticoid sclerosis, 42

Neurotransmitters, 26, 39, 78,
    79
Niacin, 42, 43, 81
Niacinamide, 16, 20
Nicotine, 46-49
Nicotinic acid, 78
Norepinephrine, 15, 47, 53,
    54, 62-66, 71, 73, 74, 75
Neuropharmacology of
    serotonin synapse, 64-65

Orthomolecular, 1-2, 58

Pantothenic acid, 47
P5P, 16, 55
Parkinson's disease, 58, 74

PCP, 14
PEA, 69
Peripheral neuropathy, 59
Pfeiffer's Law, 10
Phenylalanine, 62-73, 77
Phenylethylamine (PEA), 69
Phenylketonuria (PKU), 72
Phenylpropanolamine, 10, 75
Premenstrual Syndrome
  (PMS), 72
Post-trauma, 27
Pyrixidone, 47

Recovery time, 18-32
Reduction procedures, 22-23
Riboflavin, 43

Serotonin, 47, 53, 54, 75-76
Siberian Ginseng, 17, 75
Side effects of,
  antidepressants, 18
  pain medication, 18
  tranquilizers, 18
Social pharmacology, 22
Stress/anxiety formula, 49, 52
Stress reactions, 27-28

Taurine, 83-84
Tetrahydroisoquinolines
  (TIQ's), 70
Thiamine, 42, 43, 47, 51
Tofranil (Imipramine), 78
Tranquilizers, 5, 18, 26-27, 85
Tranxene, 10
Tricyclics, 71-72
Triglycerides, 42
Tobacco, 13, 46-49
Tryptophan, 16, 20, 44, 45,
  54, 75-79
Tyrosine, 63, 66, 73-75, 77,
  78

Unipolar depression, 65, 76

Valine, 55, 77
Valium, 10, 23
Vasopressin, 47

Vitamin A, 43, 47
Vitamin C, 29, 43, 47, 81
Vitamin E, 29, 47
Vitamin K, 43
Vitamin deficiencies,
  symptoms of, 90-99

Wernicke's disease, 42
Withdrawal
  barbiturates, 25
  by addictive substance,
    23-25
  alcohol, 24
  caffeine, 24
  heroin, 25
  marijuana, 25
  medications, all types, 23-24
  nicotine, 25, 48
  procedures, 22-23, 30-31
  sugar, 25
  symptoms, 23-25

Xanax, 10, 58
Xanthine, 50

Zinc, 42, 44

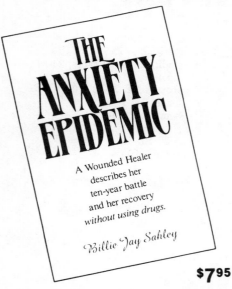

AMINO ACIDS FOR PAIN & STRESS THERAPY

AMINO ACIDS FOR PAIN & STRESS THERAPY

by Drs. Billie J. Sahley and Katherine M. Birkner, orthomolecular therapists, researchers, and clinicians at the Pain & Stress Center. Dr. Sahley is author of the best selling book, **The Anxiety Epidemic**.

Most people when faced with an illness or stress related problem such as anxiety, depression, pain, or grief turn to a drug for relief. They don't want the side effects or possible addiction, but they feel there is <u>no</u> alternative.

THERE ARE NATURAL ALTERNATIVES!!

Amino acids are a natural alternative. Research has shown amino acids are being used successfully in the treatment of pain, depression, insomnia, anxiety, or addiction. Clinical studies done at the Pain & Stress Therapy Center in San Antonio with patients over a five year period showed excellent results.

This cassette tape will present an easy to understand information for the lay person as to how much and what amino acids they should use. The presentation incorporates work done by some of the best clinicians in the country. **This tape is an investment in your health!!**

TO ORDER : book $ 7.95
 tape $10.00 or **TX Residents Add 8% Tax**
 both $15.00

Please include $2 for postage and handling. Send to:

Pain & Stress Therapy Center
5282 Medical Drive, Suite 160
San Antonio, Texas 78229

Name_____

Address_____

City/State_____Zip_____

Volume discounts available request.

The *NATURAL* Way To

CONTROL HYPERACTIVITY

With Amino Acids
and Nutrient Therapy

by Billie Jay Sahley, Ph.D.

Author of *The Anxiety Epidemic*

SELF-HELP PRODUCTS

For a complete catalog of products, cassette tapes, and books that will help you and your child, write:

THE PAIN & STRESS THERAPY CENTER
5282 Medical Drive Suite 160
San Antonio, TX 78229-6043

or call (512) 696-1674 Monday through Thursday 9 A.M.- 5 P.M.—Friday until 3 P.M.

To discuss particular problems regarding you or your child, telephone consultations can be arranged by appointment *only*. Call for an appointment time.

The Pain & Stress Therapy Center offers a comprehensive series of Health Educators Reports. These reports are researched and prepared by Antonio L. Ruiz, M.D., Billie J. Sahley, Ph.D., and Katherine M. Birkner, C.R.N.A., Ph.D. Some examples of the reports include:

Stress, Addiction and Amino Acid Deficiencies
Stress, Menopause and Amino Acid Therapy
GABA, The Brain and Behavior
How Your Brain Affects P.M.S.
DLPA for Chronic Pain and Depression

Write the Center for a complete list.

ABOUT THE AUTHORS

Billie J. Sahley, Ph.D. is Executive Dieector of the Pain &
Stress Therapy Center and Nutrition and Vitamin Center of
San Antonio. She is a Board Certified Medical Psychother-
apist/Behavior Therapist, Certified Nutritional Consultant,
Registered Massage Therapist, and an Orthomolecular
Therapist. Dr. Sahley is a graduate of the University of
Texas, Clayton University School of Behavioral Medicine,
and U.C.L.A. School of Integral Medicine. Additionally, she
has studied advanced nutritional biochemistry through Jef-
frey Bland, Ph.D., Director of HealthComm and Chairman
of the Department of Nutritional Medicine at John Bastyr
College. She is a member of the Huxley Founda-
tion/Academy of Psychosomatic Medicine, North American
Nutrition and Preventive Medicine Association. In addition,
she holds memberships in the Sports Medicine Foundation,
American Association of Hypnotherapists, and the American
Mental Health Counselors Association. She is also on the
Scientific and Medical Advisory Board for Inter-Cal Cor-
poration. Dr. Sahley is author of *The Anxiety Epidemic,* and
*The Natural Way to Control Hyperactivity with Amino Acid
and Nutrient Therapy.* Currently, Dr. Sahley is working on
her fourth book with Dr. Kathy Birkner on *Pain Control
Without Drugs.*

Kathy Birkner is a Pain Therapist at the Pain & Stress Therapy Center in San Antonio. She is a Registered Nurse, Certified Registered Nurse Anesthetist, Registered Massage Therapist, and Orthomolecular Therapist. She attended Brackenridge Hospital School of Nursing, University of Texas at Austin, Southwest Missouri State University, and Clayton University. She holds degrees in nursing, nutrition, and behavior therapy. Dr. Birkner has done graduate studies through the Center for Integral Medicine and U.C.L.A. Medical School under the direction of Dr. David Bresler. Additionally, she has studied advanced nutritional biochemistry through Jeffrey Bland, Ph.D., Director of HealthComm and Chairman of the Department of Nutritional Medicine at John Bastyr College. She is a member of the American Association of Nurse Anesthetists, Texas Association of Nurse Anesthetists, Huxley Foundation/Academy of Orthomolecular Medicine, American Association of Counseling and Development, North American Nutrition and Preventive Medicine Association, and American Professional Massage Therapists and Bodyworkers Association. She is author of *Breaking Your Sugar Habit Cookbook* and co-author with Dr. Sahley of the audio cassette tape, *Amino Acids for Pain and Stress.*